A Journey of Faith and Dreams

The Lives of Alois & Ursula Schill

Rüder Schill

A Journey of Faith and Dreams: the Lives of Alois and Ursula Schill
Rüder Schill

Published by Classic Author and Publishing Services Pty Ltd.
Imprint of JoJo Publishing.
First published 2015

'Yarra's Edge'
2203/80 Lorimer Street
Docklands VIC 3008
Australia

Email: admin@classic-jojo.com or visit www.classic-jojo.com

Copyright © 2015 Rüder Schill

ISBN: 9780987192783

All rights reserved. No part of this publication may be reproduced, stored in a retrieval system, or transmitted in any form or by any means electronic, mechanical, photocopying, recording or otherwise without the prior permission of the author.

The information, views, opinions and visuals expressed in this publication are solely those of the author(s) and do not reflect those of the publisher. The publisher disclaims any liabilities or responsibilities whatsoever for any damages, libel or liabilities arising directly or indirectly from the contents of this publication.

JoJo Publishing

Editor: Merryl Scott
Designer / typesetter: Working Type Studio (www.workingtype.com.au)
Printed by Lightning Source

Contents

- 1: Alois Schill, 1899 – 1984 1
- 2: Ursula Erath, 1909 – 2007 13
- 3: Alois Goes to Mexico, 1926 21
- 4: Time to Find a Wife, 1934 – 1935 29
- 5: Married Life, 1936 – 1937 33
- 6: A Son is Born, 1938 39
- 7: Lactose Factory in War Time, 1939 – 1948 45
- 8: Alois, the Entrepreneur, 1950 – 1984 51
- 9: Raising the Family, 1944 – 1962 59
- 10: College Days, 1956 – 1970+ 63
- 11: First Travel out of Mexico — 1964 – 66 71
- 12: First Grandchildren, 1967 – 70 83
- 13: Family Grows, 1971 – 80+ 95
- 14: Empty Nesters, 1981 – 84 107
- 15: Transitory Years, 1985 – 2007 117
- 16: Recollections:
  - Rüder Schill 131
  - Ann Schill 140
  - Wolfgang Ertle 142
  - Elena Schill 144
  - Greg Schill 148
  - Chris Whetten 149
  - Rosie Renouf 150
  - Gary Schill 153
  - Theresa Reed 156
  - Susan Griffin 158
  - Katherine Bess 160
  - Jennie Schill 164
  - Mary Ann Schill 165
- Appendices 169
- Acknowledgements 177
- Epilogue 179

Chapter 1

Alois Schill, 1899 – 1984

Winterstettenstadt Town Marker

Benedikt Schill was born on March 26, 1852 in Ellwangen, which is located north-east of Stuttgart and south-east of Heilbronn. Benedikt moved to Winterstettenstadt taking with him not much more than a bed and a dresser. This dresser was handed down to his son, Joseph Anton Schill, who in turn passed it on to his son Otto Schill. Shortly after World War II ended, someone offered Otto 9000 marks for the dresser. Mathilde, his wife, would have sold the dresser at the blink of an eye, as times were hard and they could have used the money. However, Otto refused to sell the dresser and told Mathilde that there would be hell to pay if she sold it behind his back.

Benedikt Schill
1926

Winterstettenstadt

Benedikt's Dresser

Rosa Hepp was born in Schussenried on August 30, 1856. Benedikt and Rosa were married on April 19, 1880 in Winterstettenstadt, where they settled and raised thirteen children. He was a very strict father, who utilized corporal punishment freely to keep his children in line. The youngest of these children was Alois Schill (my father), born on May 14, 1899.

Rosa Schill 1926

Heiratsurkunde

(Standesamt) Winterstettenstadt _____ Nr. 1/1880

Der *Schuhmacher Benedikt Schill, Rutsliff* _____, wohnhaft in Winterstettenstadt _____,

geboren am 16. März 1857 _____ in *Müder* _____

(Standesamt) _____ Nr. _____), und

die *Rosa Fryg, Rutsliff* _____

_____ wohnhaft in *Schuppenried* _____

geboren am 30. August 1856 _____ in *Schuppenried* _____

(Standesamt) _____ Nr. _____),

haben am 19. April 1880 _____ vor dem Standesamt

Winterstettenstadt _____ die Ehe geschlossen.

Vater des Mannes: *Johann Schill, Bauer* _____

Mutter des Mannes: *Magdalena geb. Römer* _____

Vater der Frau: *Johann Jakob Fryg, Schuhmacher* _____

Mutter der Frau: *Josefa geb. Felder* _____

Vermerke: _____

Winterstettenstadt, den 19. September 1940

Der Standesbeamte

Munth

Eheschließung der Eltern:

des Mannes am _____ (Standesamt) _____ Nr. _____)

der Frau am _____ (Standesamt) _____ Nr. _____)

Vordruck B 151. Heiratsurkunde (mit Elternangabe) 1938.
Verlag für Standesamtswesen G. m. b. H. in Berlin SW 61, Gitschiner Str. 109.

Benedikt & Rosa Marriage Certificate

Schill Family picture. Alois 3rd from left.

Benedikt was a blacksmith with his blacksmith shop in the lower part of their home. It has been said that he was a big, strong man who feared nothing — man or beast. His presence was always felt not only due to his size, but also because of his commanding voice, and he was looked to as a leader in his community. Once at a fair in Schussenried, there was a lifting contest which he easily won by lifting a large anvil all by himself. On another occasion, about 35 Gypsies were camped outside of Winterstettenstadt terrorizing the local farmers. Some of the locals called on Benedikt and asked if he could help remedy the situation. So he disappeared into his shop, emerging with a long iron rod bearing a red-hot tip. He got on his horse and quickly rode to and through the gypsy encampment, threatening to return and brand anyone who continued to bother the locals. As the story is told, by the next morning the Gypsies had broken camp, never to return to Winterstettenstadt.

Schill home and blacksmith shop ca 1910

Street view with Schill home and blacksmith shop in background ca 1910

Original Anvil from blacksmith shop with Benedikt's brand.

Since Alois was the youngest in the family and his mother was already 43 years old when he was born, much of the child-rearing duties fell to Marie (Maria), Alois's older sister. He attended grade school in either Winterstettenstadt or a neighboring town, but at age 13 he left home to go to school in Rottenburg. At age 15 he was enlisted in the Konvikt Ehingen (a Catholic seminary) and was on track to become a priest.

Alois at age 14 or 15

The lower seminary in Ehingen was established in 1825 as an educational institution for Catholic high school students in Württemberg who had the intention of becoming a priest in the Diocese of Rottenburg. Although the seminarians lived in the boarding school, they attended high school in the city. The lower seminary was the precursor to Wilhelmstift, the higher Theologenkonvikt in Tübingen. During the time in Wilhelmstift, the seminarians studied at the Faculty of Catholic Theology at the University of Tübingen. A final one-year stay in the seminary in Rottenburg concluded the study of theology. Here the seminarians prepared for the priesthood.

In his first year at the seminary Alois was ranked 6th in his class, taking classes in religion, German, Latin, Greek, French, Hebrew, mathematics, natural science, choir, and gymnastics. By the end of his second year at the seminary he was ranked in 16th place, so it appears he may have been losing interest in becoming a priest. He was listed as *Beim Herre*, or serving in the military, for his third and fourth years. He served in WW1 from the end of his 1916/17 school year until the end of the war. As a result of his service in the war he contracted malaria, resulting in recurring fever and chills in his later years and for which he treated with quinine. When he returned from war service, he attended Wilhelmstift in Tübingen (the higher theologians' boarding-school in Tübingen). By February 1, 1920, Alois had dropped out. He had found a new calling and was determined to become a pharmacist instead.

School Picture — Alois 2nd row, 1st on right

Chapter 1   Alois Schill, 1899 – 1984

Alois in the military.

Alois passed the entrance exams to study pharmacy on September 23, 1921. As part of the program, he had to be an apprentice for three years and did his first apprenticeship in Eislingen from August 1, 1919 to September 30, 1921, later becoming an assistant to a pharmacist in Ravensburg. Following his apprenticeship years, he attended four semesters at the University of Tübingen (from November 9, 1922 to July 23, 1924) to become a pharmacist, as was required according to the existing German educational standards. At that time, there were fewer than 2500 students and 20,000 inhabitants in Tübingen. On November 8, 1924 he passed the pharmacy exams before the Board of Examiners in Tübingen. During the winter of 1924/1925, he worked for two months at the Tübingen University Dermatology Clinic, then in March 1926, he paid 10 German Marks to apply for a position at the Institute for Marine and Tropical Diseases, the result of which is uncertain as he left Germany that same month.

A = Winterstettenstadt – Birth place of Alois Schill
B = Ehingen – Attended Gynmasium 1915-1919
C = Eislingen - Internship
D = Tübingen – Attended University
E = Ravensburg - Internship

Map of Region where Alois studied

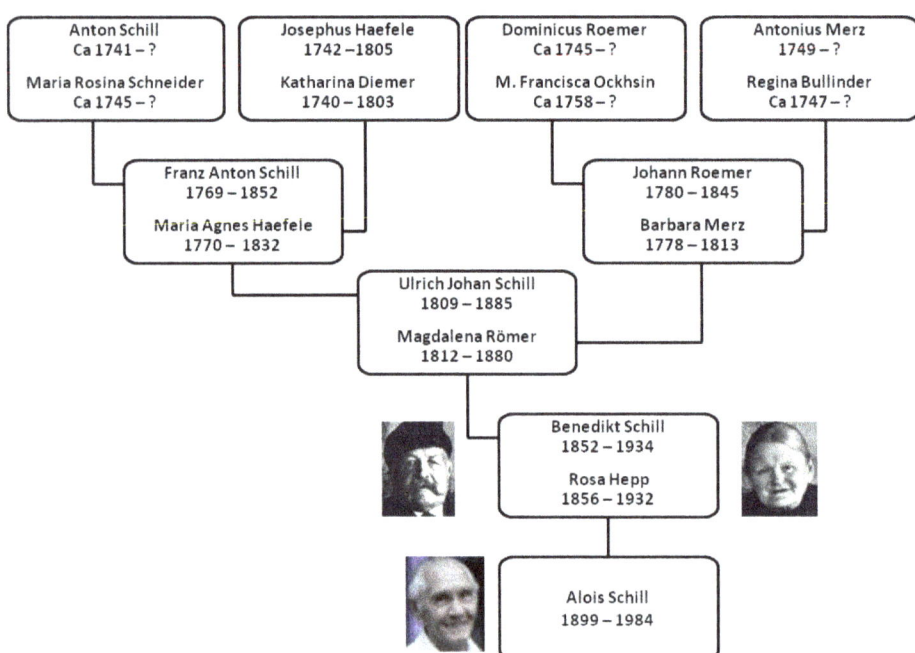

Alois's Father's Family Tree.
Note: Additional generations available at https://familysearch.org/

Chapter 1   Alois Schill, 1899 – 1984

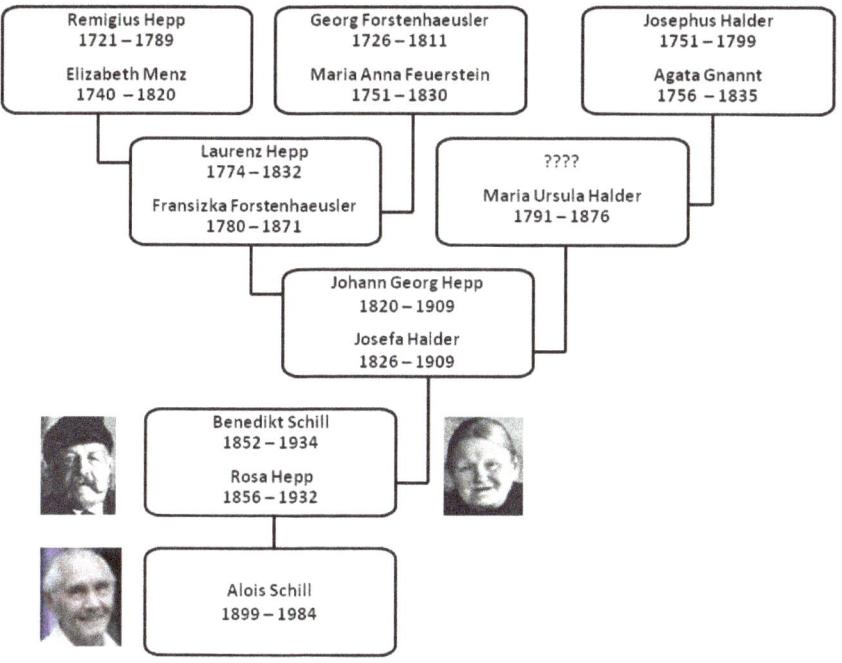

Alois's Mother's Family Tree.

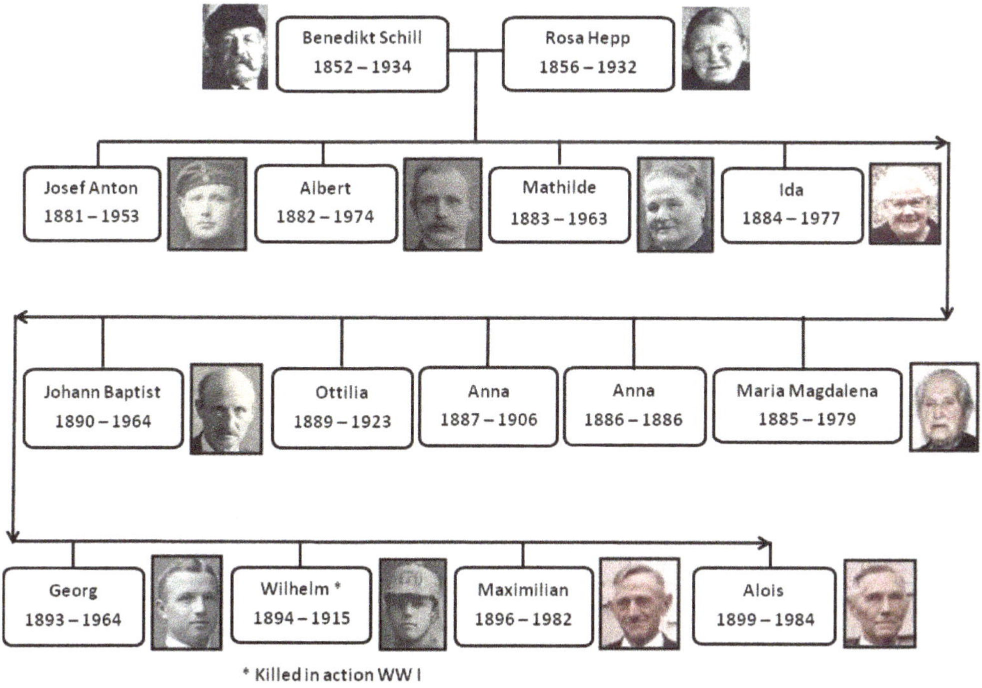

Alois's siblings

Chapter 2

Ursula Erath, 1909 – 2007

Dietershausen Town Marker

In the quiet farming town of Dietershausen, nestled in the Baden-Würtemberg region of Germany, Franziska Erath was born on May 30, 1887. She was the daughter of Karl Ehrat and Magdalena Lohner. Franziska was working as a maid for the Marquart family who owned a farm in Unterwachingen, a small town 3.2 miles from Dietershausen. Johann Georg Marquart was a married man; he had married Anna Maria Schlegel on July 17, 1905. We can only speculate on the nature of Georg and Franziska's relationship, but the undeniable result was that a little girl, Ursula Erath (my mother) was born on October 30, 1909 in Dietershausen. Her mother, Franziska Erath, was just over 22 years old at the time. It is said that when they parted, Franziska told him, *Ich Wunsh dir nichts-nur dass Du keine Kinder bekomst. (I don't wish you anything except that you don't have any other children.)*

Franziska Erath 1910

Dietershausen. House in middle picture with X is where Ursula grew up.

Chapter 2   Ursula Erath, 1909 – 2007

Marquart home

Ursula's Birth Certificate

On May 8, 1912, when Ursula was only 2½ years old, her mother married Martin Rehm and left Dietershausen to live in Grundsheim. Ursula was left behind to be raised by her grandparents, as her new stepfather preferred not to be a father to her or play any part in her life. So not only was she rejected by her father and stepfather, she was neglected by her grandfather Karl as well. Apparently he could not overcome the fact that his granddaughter was born out of wedlock, as having a child out of wedlock was very different to what it is today. In those days, these mothers and children were often looked down upon or shunned in their towns, even within their own families. Ursula's childhood was a difficult one; her mother left her at 2 ½ years of age with her grandparents who would have preferred she had not been born. Then Ursula's grandfather, a construction carpenter by trade, died during WWI on April 29, 1917. However, when things seem most dire we often find hope, although the difficulty is often recognizing it at the time. Sometime around the death of her grandfather, their home was shared with Ursula's aunt Kreszentia and her family.

House where Ursula lived as a little girl — taken 1991.

When Ursula was in the seventh grade, her father, Georg, discovered that he and his wife could not have any children — just as Ursula's mother had wished upon him. He wanted to adopt Ursula and have her live with them, but Georg's wife nixed this idea. During her early childhood Ursula did not appear to have any interaction with her biological father, but they did establish contact in her later years as Ursula had kept letters and postcards from him mailed between March 1935 and March 1938.

Ursula had a good relationship with her aunt Kreszentia, who was married to Gustav Baur. She referred to her as her *Gotte*, (although I always heard it pronounced as 'Got–aah' and later found out that *Gotte* means Aunt in Schwäbisch[1]). Gustav and Kreszentia had five children — two boys and three girls — with one of the boys and the younger two girls having been born after Ursula left Dietershausen. The oldest child was Lena, who was the closest of the siblings to Ursula. Kreszentia and her children all accepted Ursula as one of their own. Like all the other children, Ursula went to school with her knapsack full of apples, since she never ate a breakfast. She was known in her town as the *Dorf Besen* or 'village broom' as she was always roaming the streets and liked to go into the woods to pick blueberries.

Class Picture 1919 — Ursula is in the white blouse in middle of second row.

After finishing the 7th grade, Ursula left Dietershausen and went to work for a family that owned a nursery (*gärtnerei*) in Reidlingen. Perhaps when her cousin Franz was born in 1923, the house where Ursula lived with her grandmother, aunt, uncle and their two children was now too small to accommodate them all and she was encouraged to leave. Later she went to Ehingen to work as a trainee in an establishment called *Blaufeld*, which was an inn (*Gaststatte*) with a pub, restaurant, and brewery; it was an upscale place frequented by high society folks. (Or as Ursula would later say, de la high — she was always mixing her German, Spanish, and English after being in Mexico for some time.)

After 18 months or so, Ursula left because the overseer, a 60 year old perverse bachelor, was constantly pestering and ridiculing her. She returned to Dietershausen and responded to a 'help wanted' ad in the paper that a Dr Emile Burkart had placed. Dr Burkart was a medical doctor in Winterlingen whose hobby was collecting insects for his large collection. Ursula would do housework and help him in the office, as well as going into the woods to gather insects. He was perhaps her first real father-figure and she learned much from him; she called him *Onkel Mile*. Ursula said the two of them were *ein und alles* (one and all). Dr Burkart had wanted children but was unable to have them, so Ursula was like a daughter to him. During that time, Dr Burkart, his wife Selma, and Ursula would often go to Dietershausen to visit Ursula's family. Ursula would bring strange gifts for Lena, Bertha, Hermann, and Elfriede — such as a bug on a pin from Dr Burkart's collection. She stayed with the Burkart's until she left for Mexico in 1936. Dr Burkart led the Winterlingen local history council from 1929 to 1954, the recordings of which were published in 1997 by Henry Schuler. In this was written about the fate of his wife, Selma Burkart, born Muschel, of Jewish faith. Because of his Jewish wife, the locals became increasingly hostile and shunned him and his wife. Ultimately, under the pressure of massive threats from the local NSDAP (National Socialist German Workers Party or Nazi Party) against Selma Burkart, she and Dr Burkart decided that it was best for her to leave for a short time. She went to Breslau to live with some of her siblings. On April 9, 1942 Selma Burkart received a written order to present herself to the 'Transport to the East', after which she was deported to Izbica in the south-east of Poland. From this place a handwritten postcard from Selma Burkart dated 24 April 1942 was the last sign of her being alive. Dr Burkart was never able to determine what became of his wife or ever heard from her again. He later married his assistant, Elizabeth.

Dr Burkart

Chapter 2   Ursula Erath, 1909 – 2007

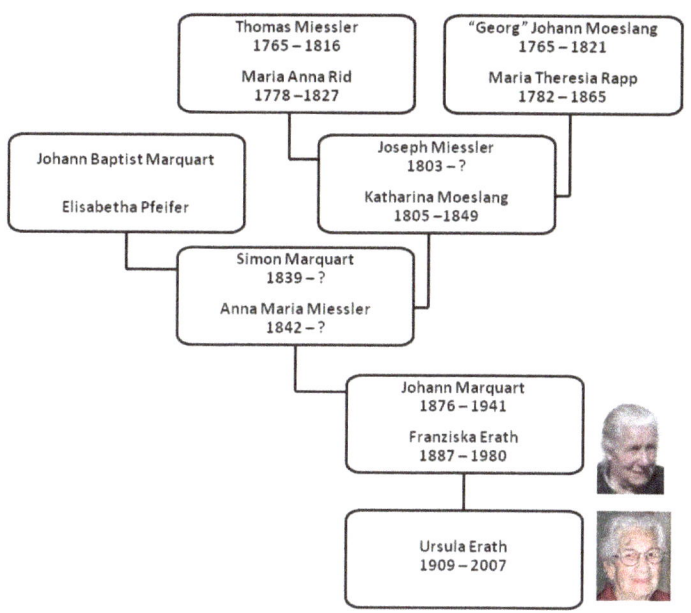

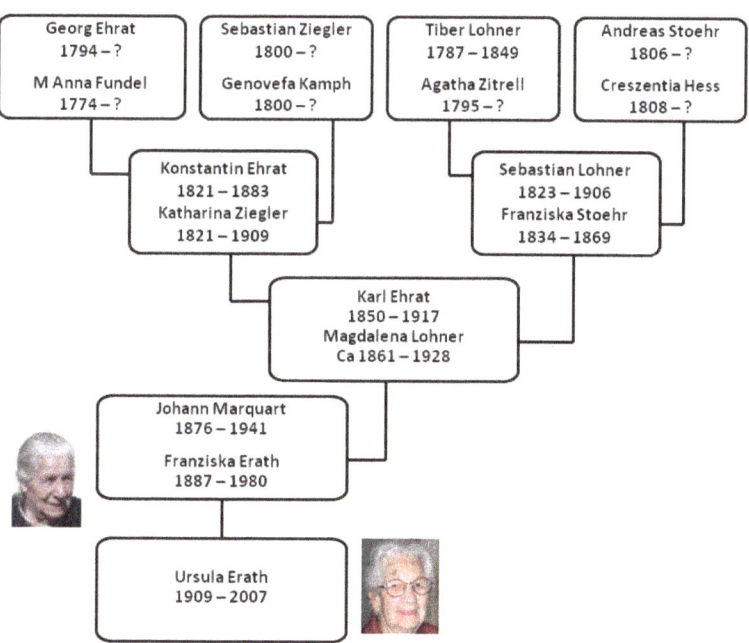

Ursula's Family Tree
Note: Additional generations available at https://familysearch.org/

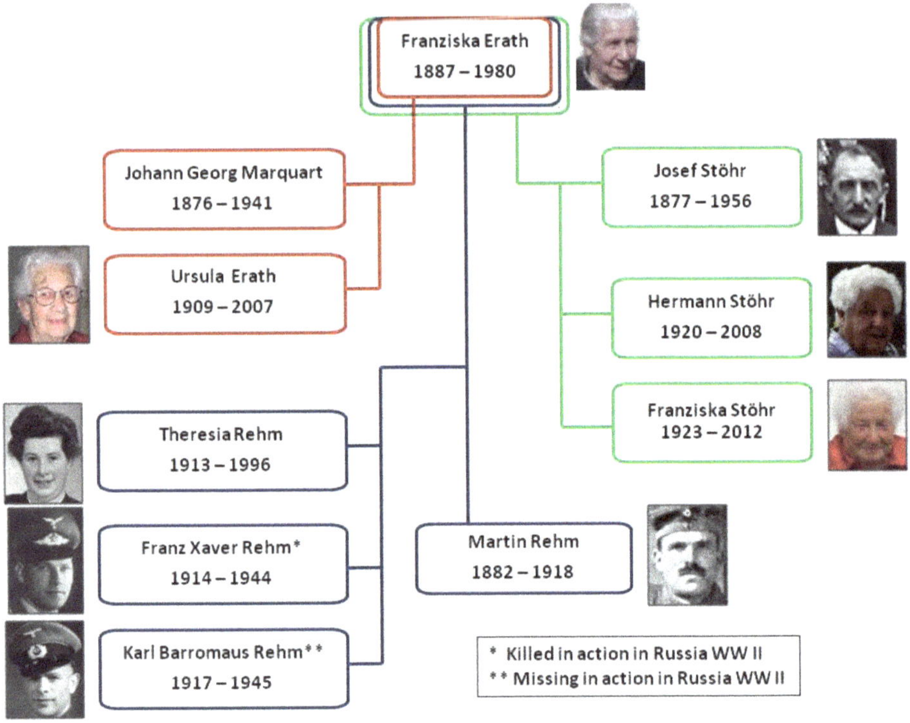

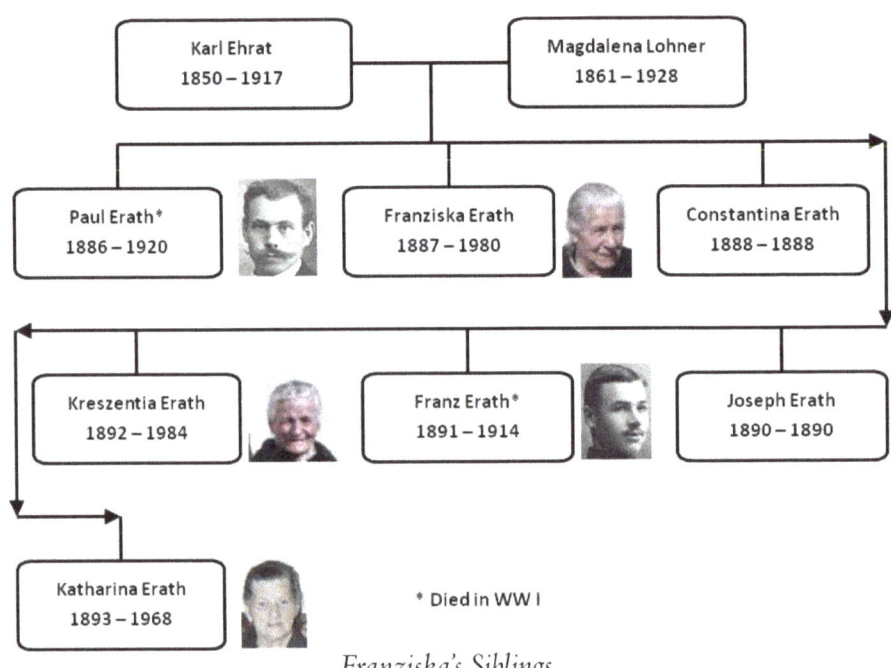

Franziska's Family

Franziska's Siblings

Chapter 3

Alois Goes to Mexico, 1926

Alois left Germany on the ship *Toledo* on March 30, 1926, most likely at the beckoning of his friends in Mexico. Whenever anyone asked him why he left Germany, he would always say that he could see the writing on the wall with the Nazis gaining more and more support. The journey took about a month by ship and on April 28, 1926, Alois arrived in the Mexican port of Tampico, Tamaulipas. He knew a fellow German who worked at the Botica Central in Chihuahua and began working with him.

Alois on Ferry to board Toledo Ship in Frankfurt.
Alois is 5th from left on lower deck.

Toledo Ship

Alois 3rd from right on Toledo Ship.

ESTADOS UNIDOS MEXICANOS
SECRETARIA DE GOBERNACION

DOCUMENTO MIGRATORIO UNICO
DEL
INMIGRANTE

Alois Entry into Mexico 1.

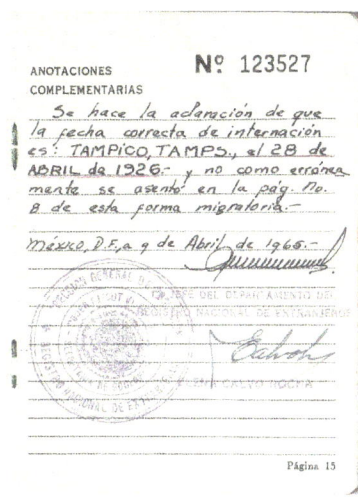

Alois Entry into Mexico 2.

It was not until June 1, 1927, after he had been in Mexico for over a year, that confirmation was received that he had complied with the apprenticeship requirements to be a pharmacist. He was finally approved as a Pharmaceutical Chemist for the German territory by the Ministry of the Interior on September 19, 1927. He was one of twenty-five applicants approved that year.

Alois's Pharmaceutical Chemist License.

Translated Pharmaceutical Chemist License — page 1.

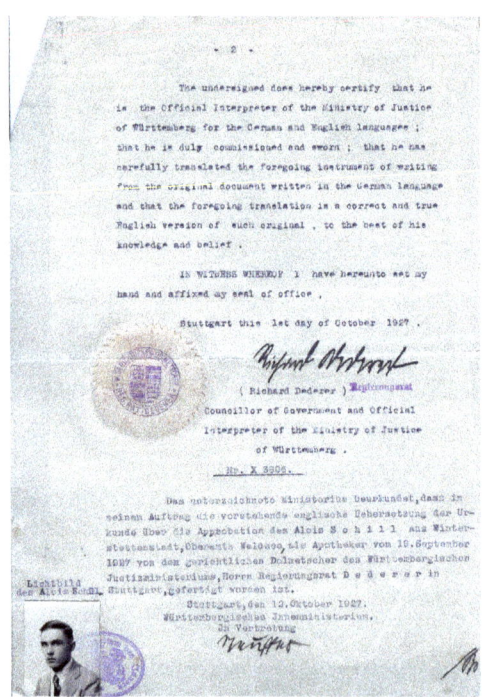

Translated Pharmaceutical Chemist License — page 2.

Chapter 3   Alois Goes to Mexico, 1926

After receiving his German pharmacist license, Alois and another friend, Mr Vegeler, decided to open a pharmacy in the northern part of the state of Chihuahua. Nuevo Casas Grandes was growing and did not have a pharmacy at the time. From 1927 to 1935/36, Alois was a joint owner and the responsible pharmacist for the Botica Regional, A Schill & Cia. However, the two partners had a misunderstanding in 1935/36, when Mr Vegeler would not agree to run the business for a few months to allow Alois to travel back to Germany. The partnership was dissolved and Alois bought out his partner for 1100 pesos, to be paid off in three years. In June 1936, a new bilingual employee who had studied in the United States, was appointed. Alois hoped that in a couple of years this employee would be able to run the business for a few months so that he could make a trip back to Germany.

Map of Mexico

*Alois on left with Herr Weppen
in front of first Pharmacy 1927.*

*Avenida Constitutional — Main Street in Nuevo Casas Grandes in 1928
with Pharmacy on left. Nuevo Casas Grandes was primarily a place
for the railroad to refill their locomotive boilers with water.*

Alois had a small farm, which he referred to as his ranch, in Casas Grandes the neighboring older town, where he employed two Chinese workers. In addition to growing vegetables, he put in an orchard and planted about 40 peach and 100 apple trees, and later planned to plant 70 walnut and 10 cherry trees. He envisioned that in 5 – 10 years his trees would resemble a small park.

Chapter 3   Alois Goes to Mexico, 1926

Farm in Casas Grandes. Alois in Car.

When Alois's mother died on December 22, 1932, Alois said that the clock in his drugstore stopped for no reason at the exact time and date that his mother passed away, but he did not realize this until he received word from his family several weeks later. He did not write back to his family about his mother's death for some time, but later wrote apologizing and explaining that her sudden death and his disappointment about not being at her bedside prevented him from writing for several months. In another letter to his father to wish him well for his Saint's Name Day on March 8, 1934, he asked about the situation in Germany, since Hitler was in control. Apparently the newspapers in Mexico were writing all sorts of nonsense about this and he wasn't sure what to believe, as he felt most of the papers were biased. However his father passed away on March 6, 1934, less than a month after that letter was sent.

*50th anniversary picture. Alois was not present.
This was taken about 2 years before his mother died.*

Chapter 4

Time to Find a Wife, 1934 – 1935

At this time Alois was enjoying his days as a bachelor by going to dances, farming, and a little horseback riding. He had been in his new country for a little over eight years and was now ready to settle down and start a family. He really wanted a German mother for his future children so that they could learn German and later attend school in Germany, but he had little prospect of meeting a German girl in Mexico.

Alois ca 1930 – 35

So he wrote to his sister, Marie, in November 1934, that barring a war, revolution, or illness, he planned to travel to Mexico City on April 1936 to take the Mexican exams for pharmacists at the University of Mexico.

From there he wanted to return to Germany and stay until August. Since the 1936 Olympics were to take place in Berlin, he expected reasonable fares would become available. His stay in Germany would primarily be used to find a suitable wife, in addition to learning about the new Germany and of course to visit with family and old friends. By then it would be nearly ten years since he had left Germany, so he did not know of any women suitable for him there.

In a confidential letter to Marie on November 1, 1934, he laid out his plan for finding a wife:

> *I will put an ad in the 'wanted section' of all the local weekly newsletters in Upper Swabia for at least a month. I hope that some girls will apply; the more the better — the bigger the selection for me. I will correspond with the girls who apply, weeding out ones that don't pique my interest and continue to correspond with the best ones, gathering all the background and pertinent information on the ones that interest me. Then when I get over there, I can visit the girls in question for a time to get to know them and choose one or the other.*
>
> *I am looking for someone that is:*
> *Between 20 to 25 years old (the younger the better, as they would likely adjust more quickly to the somewhat different Mexican environment and culture).*
> *Catholic, (thus preserving the unity in religious matters).*
> *A capable housewife, especially related to the kitchen.*
> *A nature lover.*
> *Well-schooled.*
> *Of lesser concern, but in general I have a liking for blondes with blue eyes.*
> *It is not necessary that the girl have a fortune, but I would not want someone from very humble circumstances. Such girls are likely to adjust better when confronted with challenging conditions than innately rich girls because they have not had much, so someone in the middle is probably the best. A big plus would be someone with an artistic disposition, e.g. for fine crafts, music, etc. It would not hurt if the same ad also appeared in the Catholic Sunday bulletins in the region.*

Chapter 4   Time to Find a Wife, 1934 – 1935

Alois asked Marie to provide the information to the different newsletter and bulletin editors and requested that all responses be sent directly to him. In this letter, Alois says:

> *I see this as the only viable alternative for me to get a wife to avoid being alone my whole life. Please keep this confidential from all the rest of the family and friends, and send me the bill.*

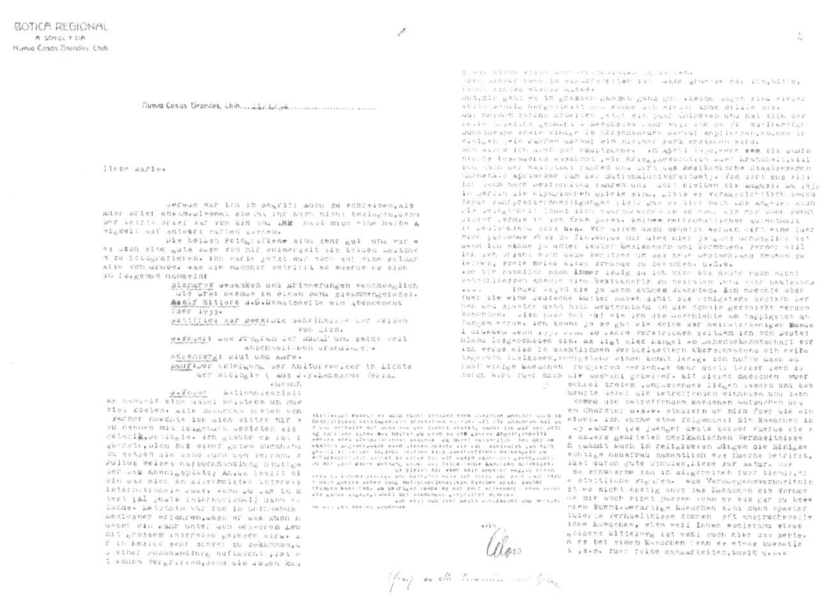

Letter with detailed plan for finding a wife.

And so it came to pass that the Catholic Church bulletins and some of the local weekly newsletters ran the ad for Alois's 'perfect girl'. In a letter to Marie dated October 18, 1935, Alois enclosed a letter for Marie to stamp and mail. He added:

> *Things are going quite smoothly with my marriage project. I have been corresponding with three women and probably soon I will be down to only one. You might even get to meet this one personally.*

In early 1936, Alois had his first visitor from Germany — and not just Germany, but from 'his' part of Germany. He really enjoyed the visit of his friend, Fritz Ludescher, as he brought back memories of the genuine Schwäbisch and lots of news from Germany and Winterstettenstadt. Alois shared with him all about looking for a wife and showed Fritz a picture of Ursula, as by this time his choices had been trimmed down to one.

Sometime between February and May 1936, Ursula and her mother visited Marie and Max, Alois's sister and brother. Apparently Marie and Max had no warning about the visit, as Alois sent them a letter apologizing for not having told them about how things had progressed. Alois had decided that Ursula was the one, because he was convinced she was a nice, sensible girl — physically and mentally healthy. Remember the letter that Alois asked Marie to mail for him? It was to Dr Burkart in Winterlingen and the letter was about Ursula: *And so now you've met my future wife.* He confesses that the only person that knew about all this was Fritz Ludescher, who had recently visited him on his way to San Francisco. Alois wrote that his brother, Max, was getting married next month and that if his business partner had co-operated, Alois would have been there so that they could have had a double wedding. So Ursula and her mother showed up in Winterstettenstadt and gathered all the Schills in the *Stadelhof*, where she declared that she would become Alois's bride — much to everyone's surprise.

Chapter 5

Married Life, 1936 – 1937

After making the rounds in Germany to say goodbye to all her friends and family and paying another visit to Alois's family in Winterstettenstadt, Ursula boards the ship *Iberia* in Hamburg, destination Veracruz, Mexico in June 1936. The journey takes over a month and Ursula arrives in Veracruz on July 20, 1936. Alois is waiting for her; they recognize each other from pictures they had sent each other. Then on July 24, 1936, Alois and Ursula are married in Veracruz, while the ship *Iberia* is still docked in the Veracruz harbor.

Family picture before Ursula leaves for Mexico —
Fanny, Franz, Ursula, Josef, Karl, Franziska, Rese, Hermann.

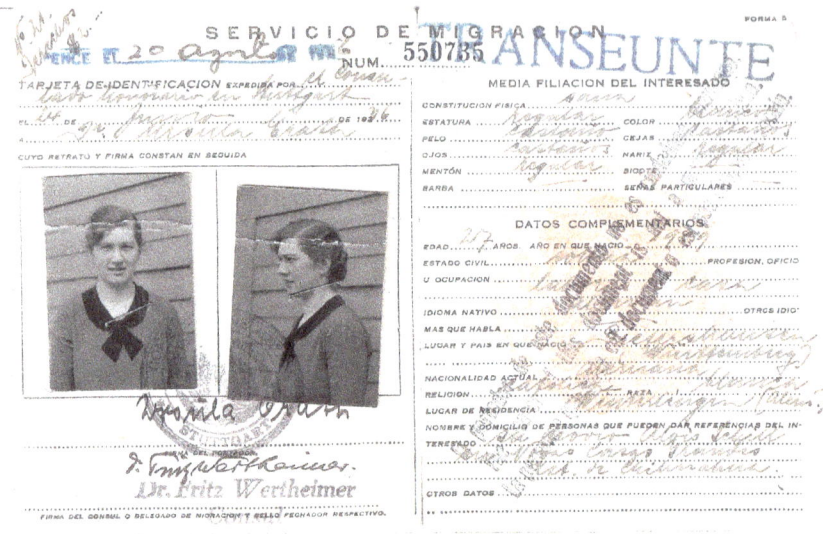

Identification card issued by the Mexican Consulate in Stuttgart on June 24, 1936.

Iberia ship

Chapter 5   Married Life, 1936 – 1937

Ursula on board Iberia ship.

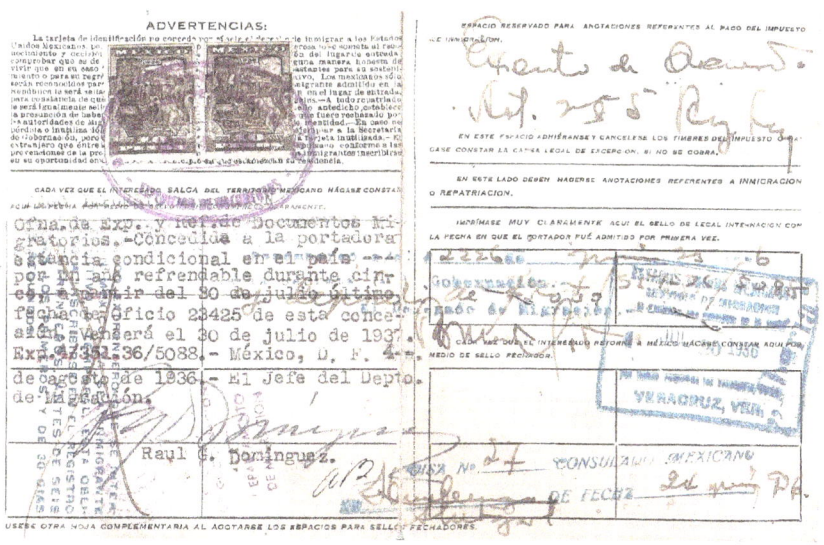

One year visa granted to Ursula on August 4, 1936.
Renewable yearly up to five years.

In a letter to Marie on September 25, 1936, Alois says this about their wedding:

> Our wedding was, as you can imagine under the circumstances, fairly simple: The two of us in a strange place, surrounded only by strangers, somewhat foreign to each other, under great difficulties with immigration and customs matters etc — but we got married; both of us arguably with the best intentions, being careful not to explain how we both got into this. But we did it! It went better than I could have expected and every day gets better.

I can only assume that Alois wanted to get Ursula back to Nuevo Casas Grandes as quickly as he could. One can hardly imagine what was going through her mind; Southern Mexico along the coast near Veracruz is lush and green — more like Germany, but the terrain gets drier and more barren the further north you go into northern Mexico. The 1150 mile trip from Veracruz to Chihuahua City was memorable. They came by train from Mexico City to Chihuahua City, where they spent a couple of days to buy some furniture that would be shipped to them. The 200 mile trip from Chihuahua to Nuevo Casas Grandes was shocking to Ursula, as she had never seen or been in the desert. Not only was the terrain foreign to her, but

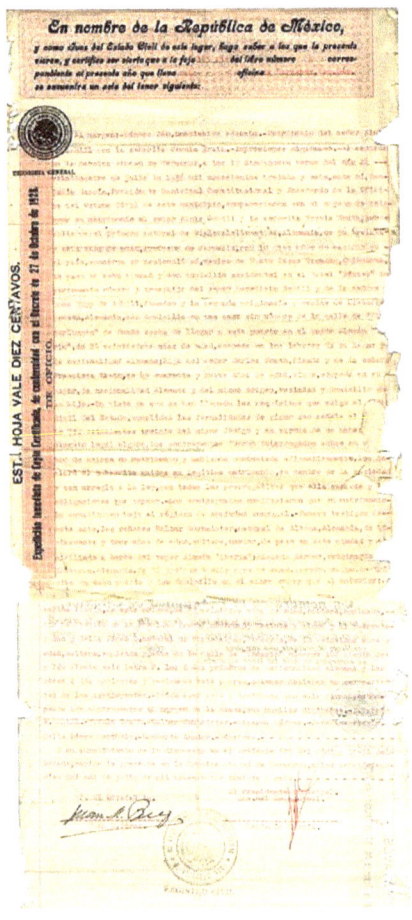

Alois and Ursula Marriage License.

they were riding in a van on dirt roads with huge potholes caused by the occasional rains. At that time there were no paved roads in most of northern Mexico and several times the male passengers on the van had to get out and push. It does rain sometimes in northern Mexico during the summer and when it does, the pollywogs quickly emerge from the mud puddles and you hear a lot of toads calling out at night.

Shortly after leaving Chihuahua, Ursula asked Alois, 'When will we get to the highway?' Alois responded with a 'soon', but the northern sections of the Pan-American Highway in Mexico were not built for several more years. The highway that links the Pan-American Highway (Mexico highway #45) to Nuevo Casas Grandes was finally constructed about 1956 and that only provided one paved main street through the town. So Alois's 'soon' meant about 20 years later.

Alois and Ursula finally arrived in Nuevo Casas Grandes. Ursula had brought her dowry, (as Alois called it) with her on the ship — a huge basket, a box, and another large suitcase with goodies from Germany. In one of Alois's letters to Marie, he mentions that it took three months from the time Ursula arrived in Veracruz until the goods arrived in Nuevo Casas Grandes. For those three months, the newlyweds feared that it might never arrive or that things would be missing or broken. However the shipment arrived in good condition, with the exception of a can of liverwurst which had leaked onto some of the aluminum pots and corroded them … but Ursula still used them well after all of her children had left home.

> Some of the items that Ursula brought with her on the ship were:
> Rauchfleisch (smoked meat)
> A couple of cans of liverwurst
> A vest-sweater that Marie had sent for Alois
> Fine chinaware
> Silverware
> Two big feather beds (down comforters)
> Several knick-knacks and small furniture pieces.

When the dowry arrived, Ursula prepared a great dinner (Mittagessen) made up of the newly arrived rauchfleisch mixed with lentils, beef and spätzle. So Alois had his first authentic German (Schwäbisch) meal in ten years.

Imagine what the first few months of their married life must have been like. In Alois's own words, shortly after they were married he says:

> We will probably be properly set up by mid-October and prepared for the coming winter. Ursel* seems to have withstood the worst of times already. The first few weeks and months have certainly not been easy for her, or for me; intense heat along with the inconvenience of not being properly set up. She got sick, the poor creature, but now her life is coming back and she is getting more cheerful every day.

Alois and Ursula standing in doorway of remodeled pharmacy.

*Alois referred to Ursula as 'Ursel' in several letters to his sister, Marie. I never heard him call her that while he was alive. He always called her *Meisle*, which is an endearing form of 'little mouse' in Schwäbisch. For the Schwaben many things are miniaturized by adding 'le' to the end of words. In Germany, everyone referred to her as *Usche* or *Uschi*. Mom always called Dad 'Ali'.

Chapter 6

A Son is Born, 1938

The first year for the newlyweds must have been a difficult one for them — especially for Ursula. In a letter Alois wrote to Marie on December 15, 1937, he indicated that he had sold his 'ranch' in order to dedicate more time and effort to the pharmacy and to fixing up their living space. He writes that for fun, he obtained a fawn for Ursula which they kept in their back yard. They had a lot of fun with the fawn during the past year but it was now almost 1½ years old and old enough to want to start its own family. Since this was not possible in their back yard, the deer's mood was getting worse every day. Alois wrote: *We are going to let him go free so that he can find himself a mate.*

Alois, Ursula, and Esperanza Parra with dog and fawn.

It was originally planned to send Ursula to Germany in January by herself to deliver their first child, but a translation of Alois's letter to Marie upon Gerhard's birth, shows his great excitement and thoughts.

> *Dear Marie,*
> *It is urgent that I write to you today for you shall be the first to learn what has happened to us. I wanted to send Ursula to Germany to give birth to our child. They were to go on the Orinoco ship on December 27, but the closer the time came to travel, the more uneasy I became, as I worried at the thought of the arduous journey on a ship to Germany, even for healthy men. I finally gave up on the plan, but decided to send them to the private clinic of Dr Gutierrez in Chihuahua, as I feared that they could be missing out on something here when the time came. In August, Dr Gutierrez examined her and determined that she was in her second to third month and we made an appointment to return to Chihuahua after the New Year but things happened much differently than expected. On Thursday she helped me as always in the pharmacy and then planted some tubers in the afternoon, which had arrived from Stuttgart. In the evening I gave her a mild laxative, but in the night the perfect storm burst on us; it was horrible, just horrible. She could not stand, sit, nor lie; one spasm after another. As much as I hated to, by 2 o'clock in the morning I had to leave her alone to seek help. I found a young doctor just leaving a party who came and determined that she had some kind of weakness of the nerves and prescribed a medicine that I prepared and gave to her. But all was in vain; she could not keep anything down. I called the doctor again who made a thorough examination and determined that the baby was almost ready to be delivered. This could be serious — a delivery at 7–8 months! The doctor left and came back at 9 o'clock, but in the meantime I had located a midwife (Mrs Hardy[2]) and now the show started. The contractions were stronger, and without any injection at 11 o'clock, a splendid lad was born — 9 pounds, 20 .5 inches long — no tear, no bleeding; the baby was fully developed. We all made mistakes — the Chihuahua doctor's estimate, the local doctor's first determination, as well as the two of us.*
> *Today, three days after childbirth, mother is without fever, with*

Chapter 6   A Son is Born, 1938

normal heart rate, very slight serous secretions, and excellent appetite. The little one is in excellent shape, being full of life and health and regularly gets his mother's milk. When he wakes up at night and makes a racket, which is rare, a couple of teaspoons of mint tea are enough to quiet him down. Mother is now in her snow-white bed and shines like a cockchafer (a rare bug found only in south-western Germany) with bliss and next to her is the little guy, sleeping or waiting until it is time again to eat. The midwife comes every morning and cleans mother and child. Later a laundry woman comes every day because there is now a lot of laundry and our housemaid cannot do everything by herself.

I still cannot comprehend that everything happened so quickly and smoothly. I believe that her constant working in the pharmacy and home, etc had a good impact on the pregnancy and delivery.

We had ordered a lot of very pretty children's clothes in Mexico City but they have not yet arrived, so now we have to make do as best we can. Ursula had already obtained some clothes but certainly not enough, as we had not expected the baby to arrive till much later. She really had no complaints during her entire pregnancy and always had a hearty appetite. I always made sure she had plenty of fruits, so perhaps this is what allowed the baby to come into the world as if he had been drawn out of the bathtub. Skin like silk, long legs and arms; it's a pity that you cannot see him yourself. One might just lose one's mind if fortunate enough to see all these things. Ursula looks wonderful and her face has gotten somewhat maternal. Being married is more beautiful than a bachelor's life, but the absolute luck comes with the first child.

What we are now missing is a baby carrier, but Ursula's aunt (Gotte) wrote that she will send one. We have received all kinds of attention from everyone in the entire village. The wife of the doctor visited us this morning and took measurements to knit a bonnet and jacket for the baby. Mrs Wagner [3] *(an American of German descent) was also here yesterday and wants to bake Ursula some good bread. The baby is no longer losing but is gaining weight and has red cheeks like a 'prachtkerl' (splendid fellow).*

His name is Gerhard — Ursula told me a few hours after the event when I came into the room, and so he will now be named. *Next month we want to baptize him when a priest is expected to come into town and thereby take care of our other obligations.*

And so it came to be that Gerhard was born. Childbirth has come a long way since that day.

Mrs Hardy's record of births showing birth of Gerhard.

Proud parents

Chapter 6   A Son is Born, 1938

Life for Ursula was not all roses and understandably she missed her homeland and environment. In a letter on December 16, 1938 from Alois to Marie, he sends season's greetings to all the relatives. He says they are doing very well, but from his letter it is obvious that Ursula is having a very hard time adjusting to living in Mexico. He writes:

We have big plans for next year. After having sold the 'ranch' a year ago, we also want to sell our pharmacy here in Nuevo Casas Grandes. We are becoming sick of being cut off from the civilized world and it is gradually depressing us. Day by day everything is the same; there is no variety here. Having been here for 10 years, I have gradually become accustomed to it, but Ursula suffers greatly — which is very easy to understand. We do not want our son hearing only Spanish sounds now that he will soon be starting to learn to speak. However this would be inevitable if we kept the pharmacy, as he spends most of the day there. He should learn German, which is just as important for him as Spanish. Moreover, once the time comes when we need to send him to school, German would be entirely excluded in the schools here. He must go to German schools which do not exist here. We have to move away from here sooner or later, so therefore I am thinking of selling the pharmacy and moving to the capital. We would leave a small milk sugar factory here in Dublan (1/2 hour from Nuevo Casas Grandes) to be supervised by a Mennonite. It is also becoming high time that I go to Germany. Next summer Ursel will go with our boy for a few months and the year after, we want to make the trip with all three of us. By selling the pharmacy, we would not have to attend to opening the store every day and we would have much more freedom to travel.

Chapter 7

Lactose Factory in War Time, 1939 – 1948

These great plans never came to fruition. I am not sure what disrupted these plans, but instead of moving to the city, the family moved to Dublan in about 1939, where a lactose factory was being built by Alois and two partners from Chihuahua.

Lactose factory under construction.

While the lactose factory was in operation, Mom and Dad had three more children — Rüder, Albert, and Walter.

1941 – 1945:

On December 30, 1941, Dad was arrested and taken to the Juarez Military Garrison in Ciudad Juarez (Cd. Juarez), Mexico; Mom was with child at the time. According to the US papers, (the source for the US papers was Brigadier General J J Quiñones, Commander of the Juarez Military Garrison), Dad was indicted late on January 6 by the second federal district court in Cd. Juarez on charges that he was an agent of the German Gestapo and returned to jail, pending action by Mexico City government officials. He was accused of spreading propaganda in Colonia Dublan and Nuevo Casas Grandes, claiming that the president of Mexico, Avila Camacho, was serving under the government of the United States and allowing American troops access into Mexico with the goal of facilitating the occupation of Mexico by the USA. The newspapers also wrote that they had information from General Harry H Johnson, Commander of the first cavalry division located in Fort Bliss, Texas, and that Sergeant Jack Breen and Captain Roy Lassiter were able to prove that Dad was effectively working as a German agent to agitate the people in the region. Bryant Clark, a science teacher at the Juarez Academy, (a high school in Colonia Juarez), happened to be on the same train as Dad when he was taken into police custody; Mr Clark had a connection with the USA immigration service from helping students from the Juarez Academy fix their papers to legally enter the USA to further their studies. He was able to vouch to the Americans that Dad was not a spy and prevent him from being sent to the German camps in the United States. Dad was in jail for about two weeks, according to the newspapers. Interestingly enough, the papers in the USA did not carry this story beyond his capture — not a word about his release, but the Mexican papers carried the story until his release. Dad was mentioned in a book *Fetch the Devil: The Sierra Diablo Murders and Nazi Espionage in America*, by Clint Richmond. He wrote:

> *However agents did capture another valued Nazi asset, Alois Schill Hepp, working in the Ebell ring in Mexico. The forty-year old was arrested in Casas Grandes and returned to Juarez for interrogation by Mexican Brigadier General Jaime Quiñones.*

Chapter 7 Lactose Factory in War Time, 1939 – 1948

The Denison Press (Denison, Tex.), Vol. 8, No. 158, Ed. 1 Wednesday, January 7, 1942

Indictment On German Gestapo Agent Returned

JUAREZ, Mexico, Jan. 7—Brig. Gen. J. J. Quinones, commander of the local military garrison, announced today that Alois Schill Hepp, 40, had been indicted on charges that he was an agent of the German Gestapo.

The indictment was returned late Tuesday by the second federal district court here, General Quinones said.

Hepp was charged with being a German gestapo agent, conducting subversive activities and spreading nazi propaganda along the border of Mexico and the United States.

He was arrested Dec. 30 at Casas Grande, Chihuahua, Mexico and was transferred to the Juarez military garrison prison pending his appearance before the court.

General Quinones said that at the hearing Hepp was identified as a nazi officer. He said Hepp had been returned to jail pending action by Mexico City government officials.

Cd. Juarez Newspaper – Jan 14, 1942

Alois Schill Hepp Salió En Libertad

El Juez Segundo de Distrito la concedió bajo fianza. Seguirán las diligencias.

El Juzgado 2do. de Distrito concedió la libertad bajo fianza del presunto agente de la Gestapo, Alois Schill Hepp, que fue aprehendido en Casas Grandes, Chih., acusado de dedicarse a realizar actividades subversivas en contra de los Gobiernos de México y de los Estados Unidos.

El licenciado Luis G. Caballero, titular de dicha dependencia, manifestó que a partir de mañana empezarán a ser citadas las diferentes personas que han intervenido en el caso, para deslindar el grado de responsabilidad del acusado.

Alois's Incarceration and Release news clips.

Wolfgang Ebell, a former German officer acting as a physician in El Paso, was arrested on June 12, 1942 along with two others, as being part of the number 1 spy ring in the USA. There were also two other people who escaped that the US government had indicated were part of this spy ring, but Dad had no connections with any of these folks.

Not long after Dad was released from prison, Albert Günther was born on April 3, 1942, but died of whooping cough on January 30, 1945. Dad had gone to Chihuahua City to get penicillin and tried to return on a LAMSA airplane, but no one would give up their seat. So Dad had to come back on a logging truck and by

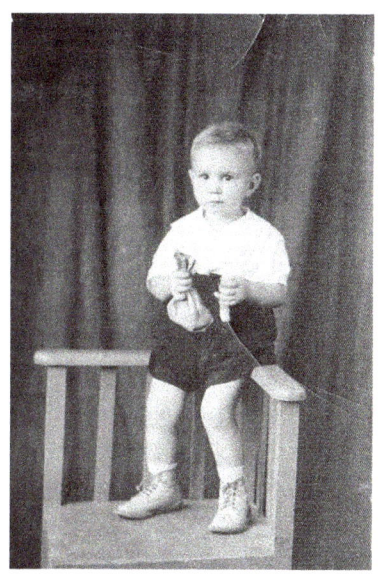

Albert Günther ca 1944

the time he returned, it was too late for Albert Günther. Drug companies had only started mass producing penicillin in 1943 and it was still scarce in remote parts of Mexico.

Albert Günther gravesite late 1940s.

Walter Günther was born on May 18, 1945.

Mom, Gerhard, Dad, Walter and two friends on our porch — 1945

1946–1947:

The lactose factory ceased operating due to the rapid reduction in milk for making cheese, and therefore the reduction of whey from the cheese for the factory. The local farmers were getting rid of their milk cows, because returns were less than other crops at that time. Many were moving to putting in orchards. With no more income from the lactose factory, Dad went back to being a pharmacist. However to become the responsible pharmacist, he would now have to meet the new Mexican requirements. On May 2, 1947, he took an exam before *Servicios Coordinados de Salubridad y Asistencia* in the state of Chihuahua. Having passed the test, he was now authorized to be the responsible pharmacist for the *Farmacia Ideal* owned by Don Eduardo Brohez (Walter's godfather) and Alfonso de la Campa and sons. Manuel de la Campa managed the pharmacy, while Luis de la Campa and Alfredo Ornelas were also involved in the operation. Dad worked at the *Farmacia Ideal* for several years, then went to work for Raymundo Gandara (Gerhard's godfather) as the pharmacist for the Farmacia Maria.

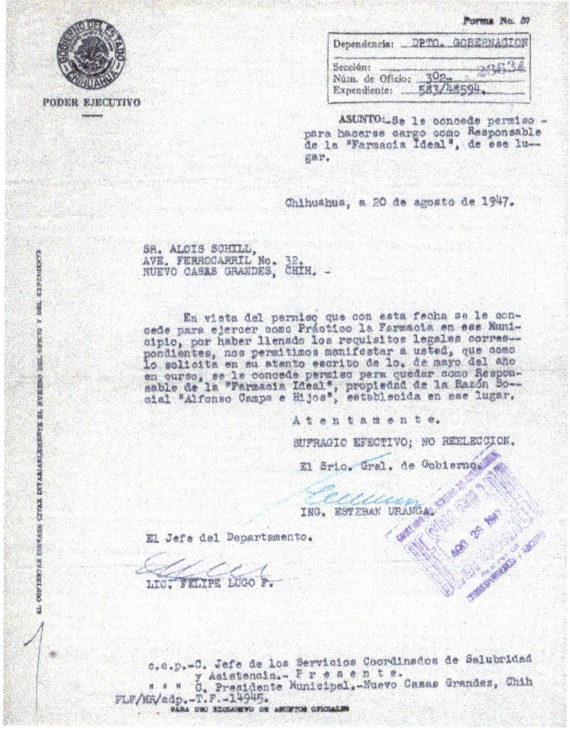

Permit to be responsible pharmacist for the Farmacia Ideal granted 8/20/1947.

During WWII, and even after the war, communication between Dad and Mom and their relatives in Germany was difficult at best. In a letter to his family on May 23, 1947, Dad writes of having received two letters, one coming via Guatemala and the other via Miami, Florida. He had sent a letter through an American soldier, the son of a German-American friend, asking how many of his siblings and their children were still alive, and telling them about Gerhard, Walter and me, and losing Albert Günther. The news that Dad and Mom were getting described the difficult time the German people were having after the war. Dad would have wanted to help if he could, but wrote to his family: *Unfortunately we cannot presently help you, but maybe later.*

Marie wrote to Dad on June 17, 1947 informing him that they were all okay and because they lived in the country, they could get along food-wise from what they grew — but that they were not able to buy anything even if they had money, as nothing was available. They had not received any of his letters and she mentions that Lena Baur, Mother's cousin from Dietershausen, had inquired about Mom and Dad as they too had not heard from them for a couple of years. The letter brought him up to date about how all his siblings had fared and how many children each had, as well as what they were doing.

1948:

In response to Marie's letter, Dad assured her that he would be sending her a package every two months with flour, sugar, dried eggs, dried milk, chocolates, etc. They had also sent a package of clothes to Mom's relatives. The picture painted by Marie of conditions in Germany even in 1948 are a reminder of the destruction inflicted upon a country that goes to war — especially when that country loses the war — with food and material shortages, bombed-out buildings, lack of work, lack of money, inability to buy anything even if you had money, and inflation; it was a very difficult way of life indeed.

Chapter 8

Alois, the Entrepreneur, 1950 – 1984

Dad was used to working for himself and going back to working for someone else did not provide him with a great deal of satisfaction. It is uncertain exactly how long he worked as a pharmacist, but it could not have been more than 6 – 8 years.

1950s:

After his stint as a pharmacist, he went back to working for himself and tried many things. For a period of time he was in the bread business. He built a big wooden cylinder with an axle inside, attached to which were L-shaped rods that mixed the flour, water and other ingredients to make the dough. He installed an oven on the second floor of the lactose factory (the fabrica) to bake the dough. According to local reports, his bread was very good, but it was not enough to keep him challenged for long, so he gave up the bakery after several months.

Then he started making potato chips. He had two big copper pans made (about 48" long by 18" wide by 9" high) that he used for frying the potatoes which were sliced by hand. They tasted great when fresh, but because there were no preservatives or vacuum-sealed bags, the chips did not stay fresh for more than a few days. So the potato chips were also discontinued after a few months.

He began providing a variety of products for the local market. If people had a problem, they would come to Dad to see if he could devise a way to help them out. When the fruit growers needed something to put on the tree limbs after pruning their fruit trees, he developed a copper sulfate fungicide (Bordeaux Mix) that could be smeared on the cut to protect it from drying out and prevent pests from getting into the trees.

One of Dad's most impressive inventions was his very simple design for an efficient kerosene burner. He used this in the fabrica as part of a still to provide distilled water for garages when adding water to automobile batteries, (in addition to other uses). He also used the distilled water to make battery acid by adding sulfuric acid or oleum to the water.

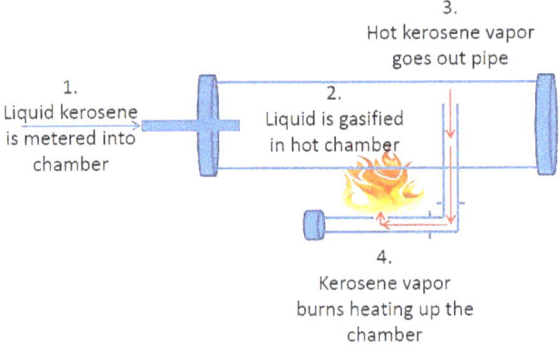

To start the burner, kindling and paper is used to start a small fire to get the chamber hot enough to start to vaporize the kerosene.

Burner design

Water still with burner

Chapter 8   Alois, the Entrepreneur, 1950 – 1984

One time Dad made hydrogen gas to fill balloons for a big fiesta that was being held. He mixed aluminum with sulfuric acid and as the hydrogen was generated, he ran it into a compressor to compress the gas, but some of the sulfuric acid backed up into the compressor and slightly damaged it. But he was still able to provide enough helium to fill the balloons for the party.

He would buy medicinal plants and flowers and package them up for the pharmacies. Some of his suppliers were native Indians who brought dried plants from the nearby mountains. He also helped the pharmacies and doctors by making Dr Hatch Salve, an emulsion that Dr E LeRoy Hatch had used for treating multiple ailments and which people still request. He supplied Bismuto (Pepto-Bismol) and Sarnol, a fungicide for mange/itch to the pharmacies and the whole family helped by putting sulfa powder into capsules. He made artificial flavors, including strawberry, lemon, orange, grape, banana, pineapple and vanilla. Vanilla became a popular seller and has been widely used in the Mormon colonies and parts of the USA for decades. Gerhard is still producing this vanilla — although he claims he has improved the product and the process for making it. (See 'The Vanilla Story' in appendix 4.)

Another very successful product was fly spray or DDT. Insects, including house flies, are plentiful in Mexico. He had a trough, like those used by cattle farmers to provide drinking water for cattle. We would bring a 200 liter drum of *tractolina* (kerosene), then added 1 liter of sulfuric acid to a drum of kerosene to decolorize it. We would mix in DDT, lindane, and whatever else he included. Once all the ingredients were dissolved and thoroughly mixed, we would let it settle overnight and then bottle it the next day. For the bottles, we would scour the different bars and collect empty tequila and large beer bottles, bring them home and wash them. We would take the good screw caps from the bottles and paint them, as they usually had a tequila logo on them, but in later years Dad would buy new screw caps for the bottles. So the liquid fly spray would go into the tequila bottles, which we would then cap and put on Dad's labels made at a local printing shop. About 3 – 4 batches of this fly spray were made each year.

Another product Dad made was a type of grease that could be used to grease the axles for horse-drawn wagon wheels, as they did not use ball bearings. The innovation for this product was the cans that he used as the containers. When collecting the empty tequila bottles, we would also pick up their empty *Tecate* (beer) cans. Dad developed a tool to cut off about ¾ inch off both the top and bottom of cans and also a tool to expand the opening on the bottom of the cans. To make a can for the grease, we would use two *Tecate* cans by cutting off about ¾ inch from the top of one can and the same off the bottom of the second can. We would then take the cut-off bottom and expand the opening with the tool so that it would go over the cut top of the other can, to which the top had been cut off. These cans would then be burned to remove the paint and beer markings. We would fill the can with the grease, put a lid on and sell them to anyone who needed to grease their wagon wheels. There were no labels on the cans which still showed a faint *Tecate* label, but his customers did not care.

Dad also made shoe polish. For the containers, he used the bottom of two beer cans using the tools described above. One bottom was expanded and went over the other can bottom. There were no markings on the lower part of these cans, so the shoe polish containers were just the red color of the *Tecate* cans, with no label at all.

Cuts were made along these two lines

Use of Tecate cans for making containers for axle grease and shoe polish.

For some time, Dad made *Cloralex* (his version of Clorox). He would use 10 gallon stone jars, add water and ice and then bubble chlorine gas through it. Once the chlorine content was at his prescribed concentration, we would bottle the Clorox in dark beer bottles and label them for distribution. On one such occasion while making Clorox, a hose broke loose or leaked and we found Dad in the bodega (a warehouse attached to the fabrica) gasping for air. We dragged him out, carried him into the house and laid him in bed. We thought we had lost him, but after a couple of shots of *Old Grand Dad* and some rest, he was fine. Thinking back on that incident, I realize how unprepared we were and how ill-equipped Dublan was for such situations. There were certainly no signs in the bodega or anywhere on the premises outlining how to handle exposure to chlorine gas. This business ended when it became too difficult to obtain the chlorine gas required. Several years after Dad stopped selling Clorox, he decided to get rid of the small amount of residual gas remaining in one of the chlorine cylinders. Dad and Gerhard took the cylinder outside to the south side of the building and opened the valve. The gas drifted over to the house and into the open kitchen window, so Mom quickly closed the window. After a few days the leaves on the trees in the trajectory of the gas turned yellow and fell off.

Some of the other products that Dad made and sold (but in lower quantities) included table vinegar made with acetic acid, pink and white hand lotions labeled *Crema Liz* (named after Elizabeth Taylor), furniture polish, rat poison, and soap using *sebo* or tallow. (*See the complete list in appendix 3.*) He also tried to make ceiling tiles using wood shavings and a polymeric mix to hold the shavings firmly together. He did two to three rounds of experiments with this, before he gave it up.

One exciting experiment that my brother Gerhard and I remember was Dad's attempt to make puffed wheat. He had built a gas-heated pressure cooker with a large valve on it located on the second floor of the fabrica. A wooden chute was built that went from the second floor down to the first floor into a wooden box. The idea was to heat the wheat with a small amount of water for a period of time then open the valve and the wheat would puff up as it came down the chute. Gerhard was upstairs with Dad and I was downstairs with my mouth salivating, waiting to taste the puffed wheat. When it was time, Dad opened the valve and the newly developed product shot down the chute and busted the wooden box at the bottom. Instead of puffed wheat, we had a glob of product neither of us wanted to taste, and some wet, soggy puffed wheat and wood scattered all over the floor. I don't quite understand why this experiment was not carried out a few more times to perfect the process, but that was the end of the puffed wheat. Gerhard is convinced that all that was needed was to add a sweetener to the formula to be successful. I was convinced that all that was needed was a few more tries using different processing times and altering the amount of moisture in the cooker. Of course, he would have also needed to use a much sturdier box at the bottom.

Pressure cooker for puffed wheat experiment.

Dad discovered that one of the denatured alcohols in Mexico could be chemically treated and run through a still to distill out the pure grain alcohol. He set up a small scale glass still and used the pure alcohol for his artificial flavors. The bodega today still shows some signs of at least one incident where the alcohol caught on fire.

Another product he made was a formaldehyde solution used for embalming cadavers for a local funeral home. Apparently one day, a couple of locals were digging a grave and somehow found some of this

Chapter 8 Alois, the Entrepreneur, 1950 – 1984

solution stored in beer bottles in the funeral home's vehicle. One of them thought it was an alcoholic drink and ingested some of it before realizing it was not alcohol. The man became quite sick and Dad and the funeral home director were on pins and needles hoping that he would not die, but fortunately the man survived and all was well.

Another of Dad's inventions was a cream for pimples (Clearasil) which was tried on Sra Gandara's granddaughter (Nena's daughter) who was delighted with the results. So Dad was going to try it on other kids to see if he should put the product on the market.

Dad would go around and get orders for his products. When it was time to deliver the goods, he would go to Nuevo Casas Grandes and hire a horse-drawn taxi. After loading up the taxi, he would deliver the orders. When there was a lot to deliver, we would go along to help.

In the early to mid-1950s we were raising between 100 and 200 chickens. We would buy hatchlings and raise them and when they started laying, we would sell the eggs to restaurants in Nuevo Casas Grandes. Once the hens stopped laying, usually after two years, we would sell them to local restaurants and start the process all over again.

It was sometime during this time that Dad left to work as a chemist in Gomez Palacio, Durango for a company. He developed a detergent product that they sold under the brand of *Nix* or *Rex*. It is not clear why he chose to go to Durango, but I do remember that those of us left behind went through a difficult time. Most of the money he made went into rent and expenses, so I don't believe Dad was there more than about six months; though for us it felt like an eternity.

There was nothing Dad would not tackle when it came to helping someone out with a problem that chemistry could help solve, as he was a very creative, optimistic entrepreneur, with lots of ideas. He had a dream of creating a whole new industry developed around using pyrite, which is quite plentiful in Mexico, and extracting the iron from it to make several iron oxide pigments and sulfuric acid. Some of Dad's grandchildren got to see several of the structures that he had built behind the fabrica and on the cheese factory lot to hold or process the pyrite and the various process steps he envisioned. Unfortunately the energy and resources spent following this dream never came to fruition.

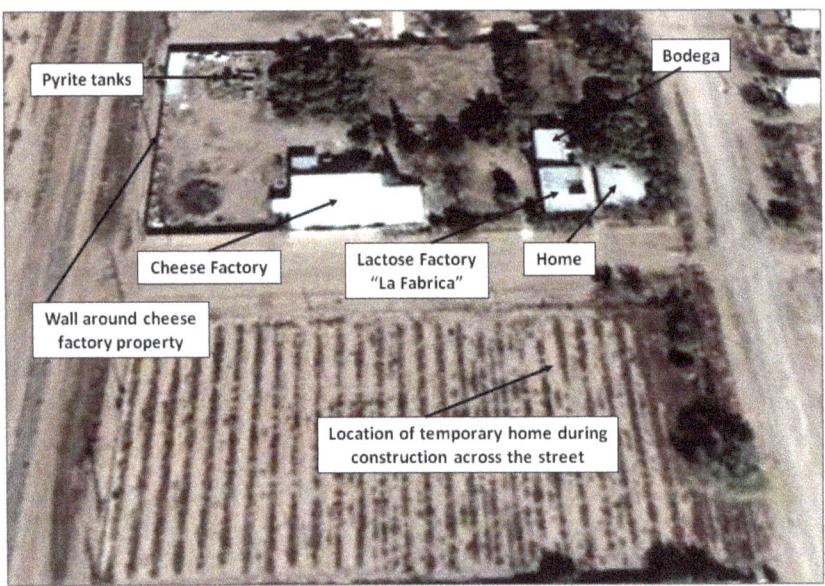

Property layout

Remains of Pyrite project. Wall in background shows a section of the wall that was built around the cheese factory property.

Chapter 9

Raising the Family, 1944 – 1962

The three of us went to the Dublan Elementary school about three blocks from our house. After school we had chores to do — feeding our pig, chickens, etc and of course homework, which was usually done before nightfall as we only had oil lamps for lighting until we were in high school. We always ate our meals as a family and then in the evenings we would sit in our living room to chat or read, as we did not have a TV while in grade school or high school. Later on, one of us got a small radio, which in daytime could only pick up the local radio station, but at night it could pick up a couple of stations on the USA side. One that I remember was XELO in Del Rio, Texas, as they had a very powerful radio tower along the USA border.

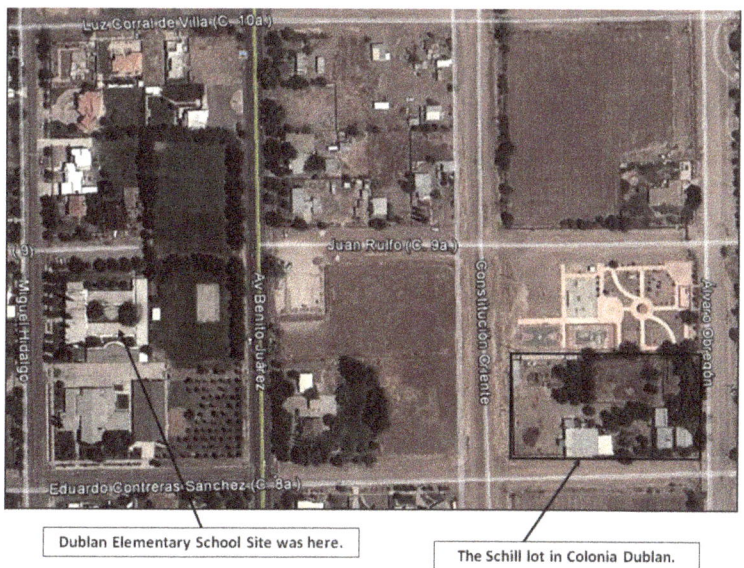

Elementary school location

When I was in my second and third year of high school, I had a summer job at one of the two local flour mills, working from 7 pm to 7 am. My job was to weigh and test the wheat brought in by the farmers. The testing consisted of determining the amount of non-wheat material like weeds, chaff, and moisture which affected how much the farmer would receive for his wheat. There were several occasions when the owner of the wheat would try to bribe me to cheat on the weight or change the results of the tests. I loved it when it rained, since that meant the farmers would not be harvesting their wheat. On those nights, I would find a comfortable place on top of a pile of flour sacks and sleep. If a truck did come in, the night watchman would come and wake me up to do my job. It happened that I got chickenpox one of those summers and as Dad did not want me to lose my job, he covered for me for about a week until I recovered. I got lots of rest, but poor Dad was all worn out by the end of the week. He later told me that someone had also tried to bribe him while he filled in for me.

Mom and Dad did most of their shopping in Nuevo Casas Grandes. They did not have an automobile, so we would take the public bus or walk the three or so miles along the railroad tracks heading south. There was a small store on the south end of Dublan and one of us would go there when we needed something small. If Dad went, he sometimes would not come home right away as he would end up playing dominoes there. Apparently the players didn't trust each other as they would take their tiles with them whenever they had to go to the bathroom. On one occasion, when Dad was delayed playing dominoes, a skunk had come onto our front porch so Mom left by way of the back door to get Dad. When they came home, they found three boys sitting on the sofa, all of them in tears. When they asked Gerhard why he was crying, he replied that he was crying because I was crying, and I replied that I was crying because Walter was crying. We had all jumped up onto the sofa and strategized as to who would do what if the skunk came at us. Each of us held a steel curtain rod ready to aid in our defense.

Our family celebrated the main holidays, Easter and Christmas, as they would be celebrated in Germany; an Easter egg hunt for Easter and a Christmas tree with a few presents on Christmas Eve for Christmas. On Christmas Eve we were allowed to go to a children's celebration with Santa held in the elementary school. There we would get to sing Christmas carols (in English) and Santa would come and give each of the children something — usually a popcorn ball, orange, candy, and cookies. When we got home, our presents would be under the tree. In those days, presents meant that each of us would get one small present. It could be something to wear, something to eat, or if we were really lucky, it might be a small toy like a metal car (similar to our current matchbox cars). Christmas day was a day to relax together and if we had received a toy, we would play with it.

Sundays were a day of rest, except for doing the chores. When we were little we would stay home or go to Nuevo Casas Grandes to visit my Godmother (Raquel Saenz). Some of Mom's Dublan friends (Senora Muñoz, Senora Gandara, and Quika Madero) would often come and play dominoes or Chinese checkers with Mom, and occasionally Dad would join in. Dad made a cacao liquor and a coffee liquor that attracted these ladies like sugar attracts bees.

My parents made a big sacrifice by sending their three children to the schools run by the Church of Jesus Christ of Latter-day Saints (Mormons). The costs were much higher than the public schools and when we went to high school there was an additional cost for riding the school bus. By making this huge sacrifice, they provided us with access to a much better education and opened up a door for us to continue our education in the USA. For all three of us, it got us into the USA where we met and married our lifetime partners, so I am very thankful that they sent us to these schools instead of the public schools.

Rüder, Walter, Gerhard about 1949

Chapter 10

College Days, 1956 – 1970+

Gerhard and I went to Brigham Young University (BYU) in Provo, Utah, to study. In order to receive a student visa that allowed entry into the USA to study, proof was needed that you could support yourself for a year. When Gerhard first went to BYU he needed $100 to get his student visa. He got the $100, which he thought was a loan, from Joseph Memmott. When it was time for me to go to college, I had a scholarship that paid tuition for one year if I kept my grades up, but I still needed an additional $300 to get my student visa. Since Dad was in no position to help us financially, I asked my friend Ashton Taylor's parents if I could borrow $300 and they agreed. I signed a promissory note, (I had never heard of a promissory note before then) and with $300 in my pocket, I headed to Provo. The first year I lived with Gerhard, Mario Blanco, and Limhi Ontiveros in a rented house, but by Christmastime I was homesick and wanted to go home. Dad sent us enough to pay for our car pool share and Gerhard and I caught a ride with some other Colonia Dublan and Colonia Juarez students and we were able to spend Christmas at home.

In a letter to Marie on 12/21/1958, my father gives some insight about life, as well as what Christmas was like when he was a boy:

> *Christmas is just outside the door. Childhood memories come up and one thinks more than usual of his dear siblings, friends, etc and about how much better everything might have turned out if one had done this or the other differently. As we get older, we think more and more about the meaning or meaninglessness of life and realize that sooner or later everything comes to an end. Perhaps we will live on for a time in the*

memories of our children or other relatives, until finally this also ends. What remains afterwards, who knows for sure? Faith — hope — yes, but otherwise nothing, but mostly the elderly, such as you or I, think about this. The younger generation, at least here in America, hardly knows the real meaning of Christmas. As children, we went out at 5 o'clock in the morning in freezing cold temperatures, traipsing through the snow under glittering stars in the sky to the Hirtenamt. At home there was a self-made manger, Christmas tree, pear bread, nuts, apples, etc. One was humble and happy; that was Christmas! Today everything has changed. Business, business, business; nothing but business! Why? What for? The message of Bethlehem has no influence on the people or world events; they would rather see a nuclear war and destruction. Here we celebrate Christmas according to the old style and this year even more so when Gerhard and Rüder, we hope, get here in time.

1960s:

And in another letter two years later on 12/11/1960 he writes:

Christmas is at the door and with a certain melancholy I think back over half a century to the time when as a child we looked forward to surely the most beautiful of all Christian festivals. Blessed was one on Christmas Eve when the manger was set up and we happily plodded at 5 o'clock in the morning, often in high snow, to the Hirtenamt; how satisfied one was with the humble pear bread and how demanding humanity is today. How difficult it is for the Christ child to bring happiness and peace today to this increasingly demanding and dissatisfied humanity.

Note: *Hirtenamt* is a Holy Mass held in the early morning of the first day of Christmas. It derives its name from the Gospel proclaimed there and the route the shepherds took to the manger as described in Luke 2, 15–20. The towns would build a manger outside of town and early in the morning the people would walk from their church or homes to the manger where the priest would have Mass.

Chapter 10   College Days, 1956 – 1970+

Location in Winterstettenstadt where the Hirtenamt took place. Taken in 2014 when no longer used.

In the summer of 1959, after finishing my first year of college, Gerhard and I went to Vernal, Utah, to work in the Uintas as lumberjacks. Jim Collier offered us and a couple of other students a job lumbering. The agreement was that he would provide food and housing, (a tent and bedding), and pay us when he got paid. We worked in the forest and occasionally went into Vernal where we could stay at the home of Jim's parents and get a good warm shower. We worked hard, taking cold baths in the river with a fire built on the bank of the river. As it turned out, Collier went broke after two months and we never got paid. His parents were kind enough to give us a place to sleep, while Gerhard and I looked for other jobs for the last month before school started again. At that time many families were moving out of Vernal as there was a slump in the oil business. I was able to hook up with a moving-van driver who needed help packing up whole homes and loading everything into the moving van. This paid good money and allowed me to save enough for tuition for my second year. Gerhard signed up with Pease Brothers, a construction company, and worked there until mid-December when he went home and worked with Dad. Gerhard took some of the money that he had saved while working for the construction company and bought tin to roof all three buildings; the house, the fabrica and the bodega, which stopped the leaks that these building had sustained for many years.

Dad always wanted to build a business that would sustain one or more of his children. After Gerhard had returned to Mexico and stayed there for almost a year, Dad was even more motivated to grow his business enough so that one of us would see a future in it and he could slowly retire. Then he and Mom could plan a trip back to Germany to catch up on family and friends.

1961:

Mom and Dad celebrated their 25th wedding anniversary in July, which I regrettably missed. I was working to make enough to get me through my last year of school and my boss would not allow me to leave and still have a job when I got back. However Gerhard and Walter were both there for the celebration.

Gerhard, Mom, Dad, and Walter 25th Wedding Anniversary.

25th Wedding Anniversary. Top — Mom and Dad cutting the cake; Quika Madero and Sra Muñoz. Bottom — Raymundo and Mercedes Gandara with Mom and Dad

1962:

On graduating from college, I was offered three jobs; one working for Motorola in Phoenix, another working for a tobacco company in North Carolina and the one I took as an analytical chemist for Marathon Oil in Littleton, Colorado. The job at Marathon was contingent on me getting legitimacy to work in the USA as I was a Mexican citizen. So I went home in August to obtain a work permit from the USA government, but it took several trips to the consulate in Cd. Juarez as the red tape required all sorts of documentation. I received my green card on October 17, 1962 after Marathon Oil was kind enough to give me additional time to get my papers in order.

I thought a translation of a letter to my aunt Marie on 12/27/1962 was worth including here. That letter provided some insight into Dad's thinking regarding his concerns about his children, in particular about me:

> *I hope that you are in good health when you receive this letter. I can imagine that you are gradually becoming somewhat unsteady at your age. How are my other siblings? We are all old now. Please greet them all for me.*
>
> *With us, there is nothing much new. Rüder finished his studies in August and is now working as a chemist for a petroleum company in Denver, Colorado. He is earning quite well, has gotten a car and seems to be happy and satisfied. He is giving us a few headaches because of a girl who has apparently fallen in love with him. This is no wonder of course, because apart from the fact that he is a handsome guy, he has a good future, but we have greatly discouraged him for various reasons. First, he is only 22 years old, so therefore he has plenty of time to marry. He should first enjoy life because so far he has only known scarcity, work, and hard effort. Now that he's gotten this far, why should he now strap himself down again? Nonsense; he should enjoy life for a while, learn about life and then eventually get married in a few years. Second, the girl is not Catholic. Our boys have all been brought up in Mormon schools as there were simply no other high schools here. They have gone to these schools, but have never been indebted and are completely free and will remain so in this regard for as long as I live. So why plunge into*

new problems without any necessity, now that Rüder has pretty much removed himself from the Mormon influence by now living in Denver. There are thousands of good Catholic girls in the States. Third, the girl is too old for him; she is only three months younger. Again, nonsense, but I have enough confidence in him that he can see all these reasons and will steer clear of it all. He is otherwise a very sensible young man and is not easily swayed. Of course I cannot dictate anything in this respect, but he generally listens to any advice from me if he is convinced of its soundness, which is undoubtedly true in this case. When he was home after his final exams in September and early October, he assured us that he had no thoughts of getting married, but the girl wrote him about 14 letters within one month. Who is not impressed by that? The girl is 22 and is apparently in a hurry to, maybe, 'catch the last train'. I seriously hope that she misses it.

Gerhard has gone back to study and is now leaning towards technology. He hopes to finish in about two years, so he is somewhat behind Rüder. I have no worries about him in this respect, because he is too ambitious to waste time with girls before he finishes school and afterwards he will certainly not tear a leg out over girls.

Walter will finish High School next year. He is now 17. He has his girlfriends, of course, but he has several so that we need not worry in this regard. Indeed, at that age his father had his girlfriends, like any normal young man. We do not know today what will become of him. In his free time he is working with a veterinarian and earns some nice money. Since he is very vain, (which handsome young man is not at this age?) he spends a lot of money on nice clothes, etc. I have no objection, because ultimately it is his self-earned money. Walter is fundamentally different in character from his two older brothers and does not have much time left over for studying. He is as concerned with making money as the devil is after poor souls. Though he speaks of veterinary study, I do not take it very seriously. He is very skilled at doing business in general; even when he was very young, we were able to see that clearly. As an example, one day he came up with the idea to raise pigeons. The baby pigeons were born here and when they were old enough he sold them to his friends that lived in neighboring towns.

After a few days some young birds would apparently come back to their mothers, so then he sold them again. As you can see, he knows how to do business.

Walter was four years behind Gerhard and me in school. He had been working with Dr Modesto Saenz, a veterinarian, while he was going to high school. He ran the doctor's subsidiary veterinary pharmacy in Nuevo Casas Grandes during that time. When he graduated from high school he went and stayed with Dr Saenz in Cd. Juarez and attended school in El Paso and continued helping Dr Saenz with his work at the animal veterinary pharmacy. With so many distractions, studies took a back seat. I had suggested he come to Denver to get away from all the distractions he had in Cd. Juarez and concentrate on getting his college degree. After giving this more thought, Walter agreed and came and stayed with Harold Rider, my roommate, and me in Denver, Colorado in 1963/64, where he got a job as a parking attendant and attended Barnes Business School.

Chapter 11

First Travel out of Mexico, 1964 – 1966

1964:

Gerhard was getting married and Dad had concerns about attending the wedding as he had been living in Mexico for 38 years without any legal papers. A lawyer had assured him that a copy of his application for immigration papers would be sufficient for him to return to Mexico should he leave the country.

The letters between Dad and Marie had now slowed down to one every two years. On 8/9/1964, Marie informed him of the death of three of their siblings within a five month period. Georg died suddenly in Lindau; Hans had been ill for some time, so his passing was not unexpected; Mathilde was the third. Dad wrote back that it was an awful lot of siblings to lose in such a short time, even for a family as large as theirs. He adds:

With us there is also news, pleasant and less pleasant. At the end of May, Rüder came from Denver and took us off to the States. Gerhard was getting married in Salt Lake City, Utah, on June 1, so off we went on a long but beautiful trip to Denver with Rüder in his car, while Walter awaited us in Denver. We traveled to Salt Lake City where the wedding was to take place and the next day we continued northward to Fairfield, Idaho (which borders with Canada) to the home of Carol, Gerhard's wife. Early the following morning Rüder and Walter bid us all goodbye to return to Denver, as they had to get back to their jobs. Then later that day, Ursula and I left with Gerhard and Carol to go to Provo where the two had set up residency. We stayed there for a day, then took a bus back to Mexico. All in all, we drove 32 hours through 8 states and covered about 4000 – 5000 km, (approximately from Winterstettenstadt to Madrid and back again. When we got home, our traveling needs had been satisfied for a long time as we were extremely tired and glad that the trip was over.

Gerhard's wife is 24 years old, (Gerhard will soon to be 27), of medium size, greenish-blue eyes, with a nice likeable appearance. She is of English-German descent, educated, hard-working, and seems to have a very sensible healthy outlook and a good character. She comes from a family from Idaho, where her father along with his two brothers, have quite a large farm (approximately 3000 acres). They are in the dairy business (approximately 250 milk cows). I watched when they milked the cows, which almost all is done automatically with suction milking apparatus. The milk flows directly from the udder of the cow through 5 cm diameter glass tubing, filters, etc into 4000 liter tanks made of stainless steel. From there it is picked up by major milk companies. I liked Carol's entire family very much and believe that Gerhard has made a very good choice. In any case, he seems to be happy and satisfied, so what more can you ask? After Gerhard finishes his studies, they will both come to Mexico. In the meantime, they are both earning, especially Carol who works as a teacher. This is the pleasant news; now for the not-so-pleasant news. Approximately mid-July, we received news from Gerhard which frightened us — Rüder and Walter had an auto accident. As we understand it, the two of them were going from Denver to visit their brother and sister-in-law in Provo. Apparently, in order to spend as much time as they could in Provo, the two of them drove at night without getting enough sleep. So what happens so frequently, happened — apparently the car overturned. (We will never know exactly what happened as the three of them stick together and will never rat on one another.) Rüder received a pretty deep wound on his left ear that was sutured, but fortunately his hearing was not damaged. He had his seatbelt on, but it was worse for Walter who was sleeping in the back seat and was thrown around in the back. The beautiful Volkswagen is of course

Chapter 11   First Travel out of Mexico, 1964 – 1966

completely totaled. Shortly after the accident occurred, a car from California came by and took the two of them to the nearest hospital. The X-rays indicated that Walter had suffered a contusion on his spine; a contusion — not a break. They put a cast around his entire upper body and prescribed bed rest, but after a few days he flew back to Denver. It soon became apparent that the situation seemed worse than it really was, because he was able to do his work and pursue his studies, but always with his cast on. The doctors are confident that he will heal well, but he needs to leave the cast on for at least another six weeks. Let's hope for the best. The old saying: 'Little children, little worries, big children big worries.' [Note: This is a saying Dad and especially Mom always used to say.] All in all, we get down on our knees and thank our dear God that everything was not worse. Of course Rüder was well insured, so that his monetary damage is not significant. He has found out that his car was claimed to be a total loss and he will buy a new Volkswagen with the insurance money soon. Their medical costs will also be paid by his insurance.

As we crossed over the Mexican-American border, we had the greatest difficulty with passport control. We would never have gotten across except for the courteous, friendly mediation of an old friend of mine at the German consulate in Chihuahua, who happened to have a good relationship with the American Consul in Cd. Juarez, so the matter could be resolved through a friendly negotiation. I do not have a German passport; it had expired years ago. A new passport may only be issued by the German embassy in the capital (Mexico City) for which I need a birth certificate. So would you be kind enough to request one in Winterstettenstadt and send it to me? The following year (1966) we plan to take a trip to Germany, probably along with Rüder, and for that Ursula and I both need passports. She still has hers but it has also expired. Now, dear Marie, you have something to read and have an idea of what we are doing, etc.

For now, greetings and best wishes to all.

Gerhard and Carol's wedding.

Top — Walter in his cast. Bottom — Rüder and Carol in front of Wyoming Hospital.

Chapter 11   First Travel out of Mexico, 1964 – 1966

I remember the first crossing into the USA for Dad and Mom a little differently. The American Consul spoke German and asked Dad why he did not have a passport. Dad replied that because of the war he had not gotten one. The Consul responded, '*Mr Schill, the war has been over for over 20 years!*' Because the American Consul was a nice person and we told him that we were going to a wedding, he gave Dad and Mom a visa to enter for a month. There are still many decent and nice folks in this world and he was one of them.

By late 1964, Dad was selling the following products: Caro Syrup, Lavender Brilliantine, Lip Balm, Liquid deodorant in liter bottles, pimple ointment *Espinicida* (his testing on other teenagers was a success), *Muton* (rat poison), *mata gusanos* (a worm killer), and *Creoline*, as well as his other products. He was also working on making something for pinkeye in cattle.

At this time Dad still did not have a vehicle, so I sent the insurance money ($1,100 US) from our accident for him to buy himself a vehicle. He took the bus to Chihuahua and bought a van and since he did not want to stay overnight, he drove the van from Chihuahua to Dublan that night. He had not driven for years and here he was driving at night on a major highway, with large trucks passing him both ways. The highway from Chihuahua to Dublan is only one lane each way and normally takes 5 – 6 hours.

Dad in his van.

1965:

My parents were busy with much needed repair work on the fabrica and had replaced all the broken windows as well as some broken joists; those broken windows and joists were there for the entire time that I can remember. Meanwhile Gerhard had plowed the property across from them and planted 5 apricot, 8 peach, 3 pear, and 17 – 18 grapevines between the three properties. Dad had been making poison wheat for the crows that were eating the peach blossoms, and Mom was making popcorn for Walter's Godfather, Don Eduardo Brohez, as he really liked it. The idea of making his own polyethylene bottles using a rotational molding process had been brewing in Dad's head for a long time. He and Pedro, his helper, constructed a foundry and made a 2 ounce bronze form to serve as a bottle casting, whereby a local shop was so impressed that they asked him if he would do all their bronze castings. He successfully cast bronze rods for the local shop and also a bronze casting to be used as the headstone on our brother, Albert Günther's tomb. He never succeeded in making polyethylene bottles — but he never gave up thinking he would someday make them.

Mom's German passport and Mexican residency papers arrived in November 1964 and Dad's Mexican papers arrived in March 1965. So now for the first time since they came to Mexico, they both had passports and legal residency papers.

Gerhard and Carol moved to Dublan in August 1965 as teachers, where Carol taught in the grade school in Dublan and Gerhard taught at the high school in Colonia Juarez.

Academia Juarez (high school in Colonia Juarez where Gerhard taught and where I and my two brothers went to high school).

Chapter 11 First Travel out of Mexico, 1964 – 1966

Walter had switched schools and started attending Regis College in September 1965. In late 1965 Dad wrote to me regarding Walter's difficulties at Regis College. They had apparently received a letter from the school saying that Walter was not doing well in a class or two. Dad wrote:

You know that my great illusion was always and still is that one day our business here would grow enough to give all of you a worthwhile future.

So he encouraged Walter to dig in and asked me to help him with the classes that were a struggle for him.

Walter and I went home for Christmas during which the four men of the family had a powwow regarding the business. I think Dad and Gerhard must've regarded Walter and me as acting like inspectors. We were trying to get Dad to concentrate on fewer products; to do a better job both from a quality control aspect as well as better presentation of his products.

Mom always had a dog and I remember having small white mongrel dogs when I was a kid, several named Buchs and one Patsy. In later years, she graduated to pedigree black dogs (Scotties) which Walter, with his veterinary connections, was instrumental in getting for her. Apparently when she worked with Dr Burkart, she had a Scottie dog around her and always thought that Scotties were the dog of choice.

Mom with Buchs and Patsy ca 1960.

In late 1965, I decided that it was time to get Mom and Dad back to Germany. I had joined the German Club in Denver and they were putting together chartered flights to and from Germany at very reasonable prices.

1966:

Mom is getting nervous about their upcoming trip and wonders if getting to see her mother and Dad's few living siblings will actually happen. Raquel Saenz, a very dear friend of Mom and Dad and also my Godmother, passed away on March 9, 1966 in Torreon.

The next letter to Marie was written on 3/29/1966 in which Dad writes:

> *Thank you for your Christmas and New Year's greetings and wishes. I have not answered you till now because I wanted to give you a heads-up regarding a final decision which kept getting delayed until just today. So as not to arrive at your front door unannounced, get ready for our visit — Ursula and I will show up in early August at your home. It is our intention to seek out all our kinfolk who are still alive and to fulfill a wish that our three boys have for us to come up with a family tree on this occasion. The ideas that young people get into their heads these days! Anyway, we have no pre-conceived illusions and are prepared to encounter what will be a pretty strange world for us after so many years of being away. Because we will soon see each other, it's no use to write much today as we'll have plenty of time to catch up soon. So, dear Marie, don't get nervous — just prepare our whole family for our visit. When we arrive by plane in Stuttgart I will send you a telegram, so you have time to have the coffee ready when we arrive.*
>
> *So dear Marie, looking forward to an early reunion, we greet you and all the relatives.*

In the meantime, Dad was not sure if the shock was too much for Marie as Dad had not received a response to his letter above. So he sent another letter to Marie:

Chapter 11   First Travel out of Mexico, 1964 – 1966

A few months ago I wrote to you and announced our upcoming visit. Since I have not received a reply yet, I assume that either your letter or mine was lost. So I write to you again to let you know that both Ursula and I will be back on good Swabian soil in a few weeks, about the middle of August. So we expect to arrive in Stuttgart around the 10th of August. So, dear Marie, stay loose and write me immediately so that I know that you are prepared for our visit and that I, with my old bones, will have a place to sleep. There in your living room, we can then calmly gossip to our hearts' content. Maybe it will be possible to get the whole Schill clan together to celebrate a small family reunion. So here's to seeing you soon.

Well it finally came to pass that that after 40 years for Dad and 30 years for Mom, they both returned to their homeland to see relatives and friends they had missed for years. The younger generations of our relatives were quite disappointed when they saw Dad and Mom: *They don't look like Mexicans — they look like us! And they are not wearing those big hats!* These were some of the comments among the young ones, as they were expecting someone looking like Zapata or Pancho Villa to show up.

Dad arrives in Winterstettenstadt 1966.

We received several letters from Dad while he was in Winterstettenstadt and Grundsheim. Mom was able to see her mother, as well as her half-sisters, Rese Ertle and Fanny Rettich, her half-brother Hermann

Stöhr, as well as the cousins she grew up with — Hermann Baur, Lena Merz, Elfriede Buch, and Bertha Ego. She also saw her two aunts, Katharina Müller and Kreszentia Baur and their husbands. Dad was able to see his brothers Albert, Max, and sisters Marie and Ida. Although they were exhausted, it was a very memorable trip for them.

Mom and her mother 1966.

Ida, Mom, Dad, Albert, Marie, and Max 1966.

Chapter 11   First Travel out of Mexico, 1964 – 1966

Characters drawn by Wolfgang Ertle of Mom flying home with her jam and Dad carrying all of their purchases.

Shortly after his return to Dublan, Dad told me that:

After more than a forty year absence, on return to my little town, every tree and every house awoke memories from my youth. It seemed to me as if I had woken up from a dream and was beside myself. It was all so overwhelming for me; in my old homeland all is so very different than here in this young America.

While Dad and Mom were gone, Gerhard, with help from Walter, was minding the business. Afterwards Gerhard had a few different ideas on how to run it henceforth. This did not sit well with Dad at first, but after a while and compromises on both sides, they were able to come to an agreement on how to proceed.

Dad's next letter to Marie was written on 12/4/1966, when he wrote:

Dear Marie,
Ursula, who is still in Denver, forwarded me your letter of 11/21/66. She will be back here in time for Christmas, so then our great adventure will come to an end. It was truly a wonderful journey and still today I cannot really grasp it. It was a pity that the time was so short and

that we had a lot of rain, but our Schwäble land is gorgeous even if it's raining cats and dogs. (The literal translation was 'raining streams and hailing frogs'.) Unless something unexpected happens between now and then, we will be back among our Schwäble folks in three years, but then we will stay for at least a year. In the meantime I will do my best to digest everything I saw, heard, and experienced there in an orderly manner. You now have lots of snow so that it will be nice for Christmas. When I flew back from Denver, the mountains were full of snow all the way from Denver to almost Albuquerque. Then it slowly got warmer and warmer the nearer we got to the Mexican border. There was not a single cloud along the whole flight, making it a beautiful sight to see. It was the same as we flew along the North American coast towards New York, but it was night-time during our flight from New York to Denver.

Here the nights are getting a bit cold, but during the daytime it is still quite warm — always nice weather; that's just Mexico.

So, dear Marie, write soon, stay healthy and well. For now, warm greetings to you and to the whole Schill clan in Winterstettenstadt and surrounding villages.

Chapter 12

First Grandchildren, 1967 – 1970

1967:

This was a more normal year for Mom and Dad. Business was good; Dad's hand lotion and brilliantine were selling better than ever. Sr Reyes, a jack-of-all-trades salesman, was selling these products in the city of Chihuahua. DDT and fruit flavor sales were also at record levels.

Marathon Oil had decided that I should go to Burghausen, Germany, to make sure that all the analyses that we had developed in Denver for a new plant being built there would work properly. They figured it would be a three month project. The plant was based on a Wulff Cracking process that had never before been taken from the lab to the plant. The idea was to take a 12" stream of naphtha and run it through very hot ceramic bricks to crack the naphtha to acetylene and ethylene. Then to shut the naphtha off and run air through the bricks to burn off all the carbon that formed so the naphtha and the air would be switched back and forth. When Mom and Dad found out that I would be going to Germany for my first time, they sent me names and addresses of as many of our relatives as they could think of and asked that I try to look them all up.

1968:

In a letter 2/1/1968, Mom writes that Sra Muñoz will be moving to Guadalajara. Her German friend Dagmar has already moved to Cd. Juarez, so only Quika, Beula, and *comadre*[4] Gandara are left of her close friends. She writes:

Ja so geht es-so poco a poco werden von den alten immer weniger-eine gehen an otro lugar, otros sterben.

(Yes, that's the way it goes — little by little there are fewer and fewer of us old ones; some move away and others die.)

In May 1968, the owners of the cheese factory had no further use for it. They offered to sell the property to Gerhard for 40K pesos –10K down and 10K/year until paid off, with 8% interest, but after further discussions, they offered to sell it for 35K pesos cash. Bryant Clark was instrumental in getting to this offer, which was what Dad and Gerhard preferred. While I was still working in Germany, Dad wrote the following:

From Gerhard's letter, you can understand the opportunity for buying the cheese factory. The proposition from Clark is so tempting that it would be a real shame if we could not take it, because it would be a considerable saving. Now, while you and Gerhard through your own efforts, have both carved out a certain and appropriate future, not so Walter who is still studying. No doubt he will also triumph in life since he has everything needed both in terms of education as well as character. However, I think it is important for the three of you to have a backup in addition to that, because you never know what the future may bring. Times are changing at a speed that is scary and what today seems to be a drawback, tomorrow may be the exact opposite and vice versa. That's why I want to purchase the property on behalf of my three children equally. Gerhard has already agreed to contribute a good portion and if you could provide another portion, the deal can be successfully achieved. If some day after completing his studies, Walter can contribute his third portion that will be good too, but I do not think that will be possible at present. In any case, one day these contributions will be divided equally. The business itself will also contribute its share, not in the form of cash, but in the reconstruction of badly damaged parts of the buildings in preparation for our needs. Apart from this, the transfer of our buildings to the three of you is underway, after which there will be a single property in the names of my three children, the cost of which will be exclusively my own.

The course that our business is currently taking gives me the right to expect that all this can be successfully achieved in a few years, leaving you a business that will be really worthwhile and which will provide you a profit according to your education and preparation. Once I have accomplished this, I will gradually retire with the satisfaction that one gets from a 'mission accomplished', leaving the business in your hands. Fortunately I consider I still have enough energy for all this and even a little more. Moreover, I think that nothing is better for an old man than to keep active, but without putting out an excessive effort.

Katherine Schill (Gerhard and Carol's daughter) was born. Mom and Dad are now also called Oma and Opa.

Oma, Katherine, and Opa in their veranda chairs.

1969:

The cheese factory and property were purchased and by early 1969, repairs were starting to be made. Gerhard and Carol had been living with Dad and Mom since they came to Dublan, but they moved out into the remodeled living quarters of the cheese factory when Katherine was still tiny, probably late July or early August of 1968. Although there was still work to be done, Gerhard and Carol were happy to be in their own place. Gerhard put in a garden and lawn so that Katherine, who was starting to crawl, would have somewhere to pull flowers, vegetables, etc to the pleasure or displeasure of her parents.

Improvements are also made on Mom and Dad's house. Walter had brought a large framed picture with beautiful scenery to be hung in the living room. According to Mom, Dad kept looking at it from all sides, with and without his glasses. Anytime anyone came to the house he would show it off and tell them that he had painted it. In the early days their floor was cement, then linoleum, so we bought a carpet for them for the living room which Mom was pleased about. It was much nicer to have carpeting when there are little children crawling around. Even the Schill cemetery plot received four evergreens that were planted on all four corners of the plot.

Framed picture placed on the living room wall.

The business was doing well. Dad had sold two barrels of lime sulfur to an orchard in Durango as apparently it had worked so successfully that it eradicated the pest in the local areas. The other products for the fruit growers were also selling well after the growers brought an expert consultant from Washington who endorsed the treatments they were doing with Dad's products. He also purchased 150,000 plastic tubes with the business imprint to be used for filling with his hand lotion (Crema Liz).

Mom's garden was a paradise full of flowers, courtesy of all the bulbs and flowers Walter had brought her. It may have been spring fever or seeing these flowers made her think of Germany and gotten her down a little. She wrote to Walter and me:

Ja hoffentlich kommt Ihr bald. Ich habe so sehr Langweile nach Euch. Schon so lange haben wir uns nicht gesehen und wir werden immer älter und älter. So Lange wir noch leben kommt doch öfters und lasst mehr von Euch hören. Wenn wir einmal nicht mehr sind, ja da habt Ihr niemanden mehr der Tag und Nacht an Euch denkt.

(Yes I hope you come soon — I miss you so much. It has been so long since we have seen each other and we are getting older and older. So as long as we are still alive, come more often and let us hear more frequently from you. Once we are no more, then you will have no one who thinks of you day and night.)

In 1969 the phone system finally made it to Dublan. Mom and Dad's phone number was 506 and Gerhard and Carol's number was 507. Because both Dad and Gerhard were referred to as 'Profe', short for professor, they were often getting each other's calls after the service was put in.

Walter must have been struggling in school again as Dad wrote to him:

Espero que en Denver el calor sea menos brutal que por aqui donde materialmente nos estamos asando asi que podras estar estudiando intensamente como lo requiere la situacion. Olvidar por algun tiempo todo lo que no tiene que ver directamente con tus estudios. Esto es por ahora el grito de guerra. Lo que esta en juego, tu ya lo sabes. Inteligencia no te falta, asi que haz el resto. No hay imposibles en este caso. Tu Mama y yo no podemos hacer mas que desearte un exito completo.

(Hopefully the heat is less brutal in Denver than here, where we

are literally roasting, so you can be intensely studying as the situation requires. Forget for a while all that has nothing to do directly with your studies, for this is the battle cry for now. You know what is at stake. Intelligence you do not lack, so do the rest. Nothing is impossible in this case. Your Mom and I can do no more than wish you a complete success.)

My parents had their own water well. Up until this time they were using a centrifugal pump to suck the water out of the well, but as the water level kept going down, the pump eventually was not able to suck hard enough to lift the water up, so Dad had to install a submergible pump. About this time the town was also drilling a well to supply water to the town that was growing to the north and east. Eventually Dad and Gerhard hooked up to the public water system, but still had their well and pump as a backup.

In a letter of 8/20/1969 in response to my letter commenting on his business plans that he laid out for me in a previous letter, Dad wrote:

Es freut mich, dass Du Zeit finden konntest, ueber meine zukuenftigen Plaene mit unserm Geschaeft, wie sie in dem Blatt, das ich Dir mitgegeben habe, festgelegt sind, etwas nachzudenken. Ehrgeizige Plaene eines alten Mannes wirst Du dir gedacht haben. Mag sein, aber Plaene machen kostet schliesslich auch nicht und ist ein guter Zeitvertreib. Hinter den ganzen Plaenen steht aber auch eine Idee. Unser heute noch sehr kleines Geschaeft hat eine gesunde Basis, ist staendig wenn auch langsam im Wachsen begriffen, wird langsam kraeftiger und zahlungs faehiger. Vorbei sind die Zeiten da ich alles per Nachname kaufen musste und in kleinen Mengen. Heute habe ich ueberall besten Kredit und kann in groesseren Mengen und damit vorteilhafter einkaufen.

Noch Ende dieses Jahres wird eine von den 5 carreterras an denen gebaut wird (San Buenaventura — Zaragoza) dem Verkehr uebergeben werden und die anderen 4 zum groessern Teil naechstes Jahr. Damit wird fuer uns ein Markt erschlossen mindestens 5 mal so gross als des bisherige d.h. der ganze Westen des Staaten, mit einigen

Dutzend groesserer Plaetze, darunter verschiedene mit bedeutenden Industrien wie Celulosa de Chihuahua S.A. einschliesslich den dazu gehoerenden grosseren und kleineren Aserraderos. Und alles dies auf carreteras erreichbar. Nur mit unseren bisherigen Artikeln allein sollte es moeglich sein, unsern Umsatz dann mindestens zu verdoppeln oder zu verdreifachen.

Nun kann man aber jeden Tag aufs neue entdecken, wie hier in diesem Staat so vieles fehlt. Eben weil es von weit abliegenden Industriezentren wie Mexico, Monterrey, Guadalajara, etc. gebracht werden muss weil hier nichts hergestellt wird, oder wie so viele Gebrauchsartikel in minderwertiger Qualitaet und zu teuer verkauft werden, weil keine leistungfaehige Konkurrenz vorhanden ist. Ist dies nicht ein Wink fuer uns, wenigstens, zu versuchen, hier Aenderung zu schaffen? Liegt hier nicht eine Zukunft fuer ein Geschaeft wie unseres? Gewiss holen meine Plaene sehr weit aus. Das soll aber nicht heissen, dass ich die Absicht habe mich in Abenteuer zu stuerzen. Die Absich ist, das Programm schrittweise zu verwirklichen. Eins nach dem andern, immer mit eigenen Mitteln, immer dafuer sorgen, dass zu jeder Zeit genuegend eigenes Geld da ist, so dass ich zu jeder Zeit und unbehindert von Geldsorgen frei disponieren kann. Nie etwas Neues anfangen, bevor das Vorhergehende nicht genuegend abgeworfen hat um fuer das Neue zu bezahlen.

(I am glad that you could find time to do some thinking about my future plans with our business, as they were described in the sheet that I sent you. 'Ambitious plans of an old man' you must have thought. Maybe, but after all, making plans does not cost anything and it is a good pastime. Behind all these plans there is also an idea. Our still very small business has a healthy base, is constantly but surely growing, and is slowly getting stronger and more cash efficient. Gone are the days when I had to buy everything by cash on delivery and in small quantities. Today I have the best credit everywhere and can buy in larger volumes and therefore at more advantageous prices. Already at the end of this year, one of the five highways that are being built (San Buenaventura-Zaragoza) will be put into service and the other four will be completed for the most part next year. This opens the market

for us of at least five times as large as our current market, i.e. the whole western part of the state with a few dozen bigger places including various major industries such as Celulosa de Chihuahua S.A. and the larger and smaller sawmills supplying it. All this will be accessible by highways. With only our existing products it should then be possible to at least double or triple our sales. Every day you discover anew there is a lack of so many things in this state, because it has to be brought from distant and remote industrial centers such as Mexico City, Monterrey, Guadalajara, etc. This is because nothing is produced here or so many consumer goods are sold with inferior quality and are overly expensive because of a lack of valid competition. Is this not a sign for us to at least try to create a change here? Is there not a future for a business like ours? Certainly my plans go far out, but this does not mean that I intend to plunge myself into whole-scale adventures. The intention is to realize the program step by step. One after the other, always within our own means, always taking care to ensure that at all times sufficient own capital is available, so that I can freely be in a position to act at any time without money worries. Never start something new before the foregoing has generated enough cash to pay for the new ones.)

Even though Mom had told us all on many occasions that none of us should have more than two children, Gerhard and Carol may have received some divine guidance that they would have more children as Gerhard was tearing down some walls and adding another bedroom for their new son, Ted.

It is obvious that Dad and Mom really enjoyed being around their little grandchildren. In a letter to Marie on 1/10/70 he writes, (my translation):

I hope that you will excuse me for only now answering your letter of 12/17/69. Thank you for your Christmas and New Year's wishes. We wish you a very good New Year, especially good health for many years. It was three and a half years ago that we were in Germany and anything could happen during that time. Very unfortunate is the death of Lev (Mochenwangen) and young Max's accident. Two of Ursula's relatives have died (the youngest sister of her mother and her husband).

Chapter 12   First Grandchildren, 1967 – 1970

Such is man's lot. We had a very nice Christmas because Walter and Rüder came home.

Another Schill has been reported: A beautiful strong grandchild, as Gerhard now has a little boy. Both he and little Katharine are true Schills, which is proven by their Schill trademark bump on the back of their heads.

Katharine is very healthy and a very sweet child, and we all have lots of fun with her. She asks Oma for cookies and 'Bot' (Brot = bread). Her father is Daddy and her mother Mamy. Opa and anyone walking around in pants or driving a car is Papa. Oma and anyone walking around in a skirt is Mama. When she is not at home, she prefers to be in our grassy garden playing with our dog. Sometimes Opa must also play with the dog, but he isn't very good at this since he quickly gets winded when jumping around. This is how our young ones make fun of us old people. When it comes to speaking, she, like our three children, has her difficulties because she hears so many languages at the same time. Nevertheless, she already babbles everything, all mixed up. She says, 'hich huh' every time it thunders. Her little baby brother still does not want to know much about this crazy world and is content with his milk bottle and that no one bothers him when he is sleeping.

Will Rüder and Walter always be so far from home? Rüder is even much farther. He quit his job in Denver and has now taken employment with a large company near the city of New York. From his new workplace, he will, of course, never be able to come here by car (it is at least 4000 km each way), but he has promised us that he still will come by plane on Christmas. We hope so.

Unless something unexpected happens, Ursula and I will take another trip to Germany on August 23 of this year and this time we will bring Walter so that he also gets to know our beautiful Germany. The journey will only be for a month. Then only Gerhard is missing out, but hopefully he will decide to make the trip sometime. This next time that I am in Germany, I hope to find certain delicacies which make my mouth water every time I have thought of them for almost 50 years, but always in vain. Really ripe Limburger cheese which can be recognized at least 10 km away even against the wind, and salted herring with all the kingly fixings.

Well, dear Marie, before we wake you from your daily peacefulness, you'll hear from me again. Meanwhile, warm greetings from all of us. Best wishes also to Max Sr and Jr and families, as well as Karl, etc.

Mom with Katherine, Dad with Ted and Mom's dog ca 1971.

1970:

On 2/13/1970 Raymundo Gandara died of a heart attack. Sra Muñoz moved to Guadalajara to live with Arturo her son, and Beula went to San Francisco to work. So Mom is losing some of her friends, but Katherine is filling the void and comes over as often as she can.

Walter graduated from Regis College in May 1970 with a degree in Business and settled down in Denver. When he came home, he sat in Opa's chair and Katherine took him by the hand and explained to him that he was sitting in Opa's chair and made it clear that only Opa and Oma were allowed to sit there. The chairs on the veranda were reserved for Opa and Oma and even her parents were not allowed to sit there. When Katherine comes over, she asks for 'orange lemonade' because Coca Cola is 'Opa's lemonade' and she has two little Mitzies and a Schnautzele to play with. She tells her dad, *andale daddy* (hurry up daddy) — which she probably picked up from Mom.

Chapter 12   First Grandchildren, 1967 – 1970

My parents enjoy several opportunities to watch Katherine and Ted. Mom writes:

This girl is so full of energy that she completely wears me out. One does not have sufficient eyes to watch her because she is so fit and fast. She speaks all three languages all mixed up and that mouth is not still for one second. Every night she wants to go with Oma and Opa to 'Gandes' (Nuevo Casas Grandes) to bring 'bot' (bread), ice cream, orange soda for Katherine and Coca Cola for Opa. Often she puts her arms around your neck and almost strangles you with love when she should go home. Then the music starts, 'Visit Oma — no, no, no casa — stay Oma'. She often comes alone when she can escape, then hides when she hears her mother coming, but is very docile and understands when you get a little forceful with her. The little one (Ted) is very cute, tall and strong; the opposite of little Katherine, but he is also very lively, laughs at everyone and has a very nice character.

Dad had written to Marie that barring anything unexpected, he and Mom would be back in three years. Well, they did go back in August 1970 and this time they went with Walter. Fortunately Gerhard and Carol were now living in Mexico and could look after the home and business. They had an enjoyable trip as the weather was ideal for traveling and found their relatives mostly well. They not only visited relatives but also travelled on their own through other parts of Europe. Upon returning, Mom was saddened by just how ugly and dirty everything now seemed to her. She realized that they had gotten used to it over the years. She doesn't want to go back to Germany again because she might not return to Mexico — as everything is so clean and nice over there.

Chapter 13

The Family Grows, 1971 – 1980+

1971:

Mom writes:

> *Sra Dienner is returning to beautiful Austria and leaving this God-forsaken desert. I would also be delighted to leave. It is not good to visit Germany and then return here to live, but one gets used to it. One friend leaves the country, but another friend returned to Dublan; Sra Muñoz came back in April 1971 because her son was not able to get a job.*

In May 1971, Walter surprises all of us by announcing he and Ann are getting married in a few weeks. The wedding takes place as scheduled and Gerhard, Carol, Katherine, Ted, Mom, and Dad drive up from Mexico and I fly in from Philadelphia. We all enjoyed the wedding; what remains is a beautiful memory.

Ann and Walter's wedding.

In October Mom cut her leg on some wiring when doing something she should not have been doing — watering and doing so at night. This consisted of shutting off the ditch and routing the water into our yard, then checking for the next several hours to see when the water had flooded the area to be watered. Usually we let the water flood the area to about 2 – 4 inches, at which point the water would again be routed away to the next property that had purchased water. On another occasion she left a pan of oil on the stove and was interrupted by a delivery for the business and came back to find the oil was smoking. She tried to take the pan into the wash room to throw it out, but her elbow caught the door and the boiling oil spilled onto her foot. It did not hurt right away but after five days it started to really hurt and swell up.

Dad writes on 12/14/71:

> *The business is running well and by the end of the year, sales will have increased 20% above any previous year. Since the entire cheese factory (ex Queseria) property is now surrounded by a wall (not as solid as that of Berlin), next year I can begin with new things and in higher volumes, about which I will write another time. What I can say now is that everything I do, I always do so that when I am gone, which sooner or later must happen, my children will have a property without either economic or technical problems. I consider this of major importance as I see no chance of any of my children being interested in the business and that way at least you will all have something you could rent or sell. That's up to you all, but for now your mother and I live relatively well off the business and in peace.*

1972:

On 1/2/1972 Mom wrote thanking me for my phone call on New Year's Day. As was frequently the case then, and still is today, the connection was terrible and very difficult to have any good conversation which was what prompted Mom to write. She wrote that Schnautzele, her dog had again gone down a wrong path and had another black puppy which was born dead. So Dad had to call the vet, who was a friend of the family, to do his magic to ensure Schnautz would be okay.

Mom and Dad's third grandchild, Kurt Schill (Walter and Ann), is born. If we take Mom's advice, we have only three more to go.

In February I invited them to come to visit me in Pennsylvania and sent them tickets to fly from El Paso, Texas to Philadelphia. I had been in Pennsylvania for a couple of years and wanted them to see where I lived and show them the area. I knew they would both like it, as it is green and lush here and would remind them of Germany. At the time I had been dating Mary Ann for a couple of years but although we had discussed marriage, we had no plans. During one of our discussions, Mary Ann put the pressure on me and said that if we are going to get married at all, we would have to get married this year. It was in May when Mom and Dad came for the visit. We had been invited to dinner at the home of Mary Ann's parents. As we were all gathered around the table, I got up and announced that Mary Ann and I were getting married. Well, that announcement went off like a bomb — it surprised everyone, even me. I think Mary Ann's parents gulped hard as they had just made plans to go to the Ukraine and perhaps the piggy bank had been exhausted to pay for that trip. Anyway, we decided that we would get married in September. I got a lot of grief from Mary Ann's mother because I had not yet yielded a ring for Mary Ann but eventually I picked out a ring by myself, so now Mary Ann's mother was satisfied. We decided that Katherine, Gerhard's daughter, would be the flower girl and she was excited about that.

There were several months to prepare for the wedding, so in the meantime Mom and Dad had a chance to visit Walter and Ann in Denver. Ann wrote me a letter and said:

> We enjoyed having Mom and Dad here. Dad read most of the time, while Mom and I mowed the lawn, did the dishes and other odd jobs. Kurt was spoiled after she left as she would hold him till he fell asleep after supper, which was getting to be pretty late — 9 or so. The first couple of days after they left he cried and cried to be held. She got a big charge out of feeding him, because you have to hurry to get him the next bite before he gets upset.

We had a lovely wedding, though the ceremony was way too long for many of us. I think hearing how Dad described the entire scenario is better than I ever could as he brings out some aspects of how it all unfolded. So in a letter to Marie dated 12/29/72, he wrote:

On Rüder's invitation we (Ursula and I) visited him in May. Rüder obviously wanted us to get to know the girl who was later to become his wife and to let him know our impression of her. Well, this has happened and our impression of Mary Ann is that she was created in the cradle for Rüder. Young, healthy, very lively, hard-working and intellectually open-minded and incidentally also quite beautiful; I think that she is a very good fit. In addition, they have already known each other for two years, so it is fair to assume that their characters are compatible. So we, in good conscience, advised him to marry the girl. Finally, he also is of the right age to marry and ultimately it makes life easier living as couples if they are compatible. To keep matters brief, while dining at the home of her parents, they announced their engagement and set the date of their wedding. So the purpose of our trip was fulfilled and we flew back to Mexico again.

For the wedding in September, we took little Katherine (Gerhard's daughter) and flew eight days ahead to make her familiar with her strange surroundings. Gerhard, Carol, and little Teddy then came later from Mexico. Walter and Ann and little Kurt flew in from Denver, so that the whole Schill clan had a rendezvous there. The church wedding was especially beautiful in a small church in Byzantine style, with beautiful stained-glass windows forming the outer frame for the ceremony which was performed by two priests — a Roman Catholic and a Byzantine Catholic. Katherine and a small boy, a son of a friend of Rüder's from Chicago, formed part of the wedding party which was very pleasing to see. In attendance were friends of Rüder, as well as a few work colleagues and of course all the relatives and acquaintances of Mary Ann. The wedding was not overly large, as they did not want a huge wedding and there was a dinner and dance reception that evening. The next day everyone scattered; the newlyweds left on a short honeymoon trip to Jamaica, the Rider family to Chicago, Axel and Walter and their families to Denver and the rest of the Schills went back to Mexico.

Our wedding must have impressed my parents, as Dad wrote to us at the end of November 1972:

We still remember your wedding ceremony as the most beautiful we have ever seen. Everything fell into place to make it so; the beautiful little eastern-style church, the solemnity of the ceremony, and all the nice people we met there. It was really beautiful.

Mary Ann and Rüder's wedding.

During the 1971 – 1973 school years, Dad taught organic and inorganic chemistry at a local Mexican secondary school, the Escuela Preparatoria Lic Adolfo Lopez Mateos, with highly satisfactory results. However, Dad wrote to Marie that he is doing this quite against his will and that he was almost forced into office as a schoolmaster.

1973:

Mom and Dad get two more grandchildren — David (Gerhard and Carol) and Greg (Mary Ann and I). Gerhard had already met or exceeded Mom's quota; Walter was at the limit; I was half way there.

1974:

Inflation hits Mexico; the price of gasoline almost triples and everything goes up in cost, with meat being the only exception. After having risen to almost 30 pesos a kilo over the years, it now drops to almost half because the USA, a large importer of Mexican beef, shuts down these imports.
12/17/1974: Dad writes to Marie:

Gerhard and Carol have a fourth child on the way, even though we advise him at every opportunity to finally draw a line under the count. The commandment to Adam and Eve to fill the earth with people was fulfilled long ago. Additional people only result in more hunger, revolutions, wars, etc.

He further writes that Walter and Ann are also awaiting a second child and have moved into a new home in Denver. Dad and Mom were to visit them for Christmas, but that did not happen because they were still waiting for their German passports, so they spent Christmas with Gerhard and Carol instead. He enclosed a photo of all of us and wrote: *… and the moral of the story: Even in America and Mexico, the Schills will hardly become extinct.*

Chapter 13 The Family Grows, 1971 – 1980+

1974 Dublan reunion Kurt, Katherine, Dad, David, Greg, Mom, and Ted.

1975:

Dad was having trouble with his prostate so Gerhard drove him to Cd. Juarez to see the doctor. He wrote to me on 10/5/1975:

> *You know that I underwent surgery on 09/13/75 in Cd. Juarez. The doctor had advised me to do so to avoid complications with the kidneys, so I decided to immediately have the surgery. It took a little over an hour and then on 9/16 I was able to leave the hospital, very weakened by the surgery and perhaps the antibiotics. Today I've gotten back most of my strength, have a good appetite, sleep a lot and feel like a newborn, without the prostate. The surgery was a great success.*

10/3/75: Dad went back for a follow-up visit to the doctor and while they were there, Mom also saw a doctor. They found that she had a slight problem with a leaking valve in her heart and her arteries were clogging up and that she had high blood pressure. Medication and a suitable diet were prescribed. Although I'm not sure she did anything about her diet — she did take the medication.

Two more grandchildren are born — Susan (Walter and Ann) and

Victor (Gerhard and Carol). These are grandchildren number six and seven. My parents hope that Victor will be the last child for Gerhard and Carol in these crazy times.

I was scheduled to take a business trip to Germany in November and Mom and Dad wanted to make sure that I visited our relatives, especially Mom's mother. Mom was glad I was going to Grötzingen as she had visited Uncle Mile when he was in the thermal baths there and she wondered if the *Teresienhaus* still existed. I never made it there, as I went to a different Grötzingen — one near Stuttgart.

1976:

After 13 years Mom again has a lump on her face, so she sees a doctor in Chihuahua. He schedules surgery for the next day, Oct 30, her birthday, and removes the lump. He assures her that she is good for another 13 years, but to get a yearly checkup.

Two more grandchildren arrive: Jennie (Rüder and Mary Ann) and Caryn (Walter and Ann), which brings the number of grandchildren to nine — 50% over quota.

1976 Denver reunion — Jennie, Dad, Ted, David, Kurt, Mom, Susan, Victor, Katherine, and Greg. Caryn was not yet born.

1977:

Dad was having a real problem obtaining lanolin in Mexico, so I shipped several five gallon cans from the USA to Deming and from there it was brought down to Dublan.

The lime sulfur and Bordeaux business picks up, as the peso was devalued from 12.50 to the dollar to 20.40 and then 26.40 to the dollar, with rumors that it could drop to 40 – 50 to the dollar. Because of the devaluation, the fruit growers who had started to buy these products in the USA are now coming back to Dad to supply it locally.

In May of 1977, Mom feels that Dad needs a vacation, as he was having such a problem getting materials and things are taking months to come from Monterrey. So Walter and I planned the following trip for them. They would fly from El Paso to Philadelphia to stay with us for some time then return via Denver to visit Walter. The only available time to do that would be in July when Gerhard is out of school. Their visa expired in August but they could be back before it expired. And so it came to pass that Mom and Dad visited us in Pennsylvania, and Walter and Ann in Colorado.

1978:

Elena (Gerhard and Carol), grandchild number ten is born.

In addition to Sra Muñoz and Quika, who come almost every day to play dominoes, Mom now has new friends, a German couple who moved to Colonia Juarez, so now she has someone from her motherland to visit.

1979:

While Walter was visiting Mom and Dad over Easter, Susan got chicken pox, so of course all of Gerhard and Carol's kids got chicken pox as well. The kids were all delighted because they did not have to go to school and could spend time with their cousins.

Mom and Dad want to go to Germany again in July as Mom's mother is now 91 years old and very ill. Meanwhile news came that Marie died on 4/21/1979 on her 94th birthday and Dad was very sad, as he would have liked to have seen her one more time; so now only Max is left of his siblings. They prepare for their trip, hoping that they can meet as many as they possibly can. They have a wonderful trip and Dad writes that it was a real recovery for him, as he needed a change and rest. Mom's mother and Rese are both now doing much better. Mom writes: *I wish I could live there. It is definitely different than here.*

Senze, Carolin, Mom, Dad, and Max — Lake Constance, 1979.

Last picture of Mom and her mother together, 1979.

Rosie (Gerhard and Carol), grandchild number eleven is born.

We spent a week with Mom and Dad between Christmas 1979 and New Year 1980. Shortly after we returned to Pennsylvania, Dad got seriously ill with a bad cold and fever which kept him in bed. They called Dr Salas who prescribed some pills which sent Dad into unconsciousness lasting almost two days. The pills contained aspirin in addition to codeine, normally appropriate for colds, coughs, etc, but the codeine was in a special form or combined with other drugs still not well accepted by the Health Authorities, so this resulted in a form of drug overdose. Dad wrote:

> *This time I escaped, but I will take it as a warning — from now on there is nothing, nor anyone, that will make me do something that requires much effort, as I now have a young man to help me. As for the business of the pigments, as I told you, I am firmly resolved to go forward since I don't see any insurmountable problems. There is already capital invested in it and to stop would mean losing all that. In addition, the installations already existing would be a great hindrance on the property, so going forward is only appropriate.*

1980:

Alan (Walter and Ann), grandchild number twelve is born. We are now twice our combined quota.

Mom's mother, my grandmother, passed away on 12/14/1980. She was almost 98 years old.

Chapter 14

Empty Nesters, 1981 – 1984

1981:

Dad was having some issues with coughing which did not let him sleep at night. He did not want to eat much either and Mom thinks that all the medication has upset his stomach. They have seen a third doctor who diagnoses inflamed bronchial tubes, but no fever.

On 3/17/1981 Mom received a letter from Rese that took five weeks to reach her. Previously Rese had sent a copy of her mother's Will but it was not received. Mom was upset with her relatives in Germany because her mother was in the hospital for more than six weeks before anyone let her know. She wrote:

> *I was in Denver almost the entire month of November and could have gone to Germany from there. Now they want me to come, but they will have to wait until I can arrange to go again.*

Rese wrote that each of her Mom's children will get about 7000 to 8000 Marks, about 80,000 pesos. So Mom will have to return to Germany at some point to settle this, but a trip to Germany at present is out of the question as Dad has been sick almost 3 months now. In spite of being tired and weak, he is still working but often takes a nap during the day.

By now Dad is over the terrible coughing that weakened him quite a bit for several weeks. On April 17, 1981, he writes: *All that is over now and I now feel as before.* He adds that they had a winter and spring like they had not seen in 50 years with nice rains during the first three months, almost no cold and now for Easter everything is green and beautiful. His business is growing more than the inflation, especially with his horticulture products. He further writes:

> *I have still not abandoned the pyrite (pigments) project. It is going very slowly because I don't have much time for it but at least I see this business very clearly. Even though I will not get much benefit, because of my age, there will be many who will benefit from it. The times are getting more and more difficult with every year and he who has the most to offer will have the advantage.*

Gerhard and family in front of their home in Colonia Juarez.

On August 24, 1981, Gerhard and family moved to Colonia Juarez where Gerhard was principal of the high school and had been doing his best to commute. So to make him more effective, they made the move but now Mom and Dad will not see their grandkids as often. On that same day Dad writes a letter to Greg (his grandson).

Chapter 14 Empty Nesters, 1981 – 1984

Dear Greg,

It is a real shame to me for not having answered your fine letter earlier. We see that you, dear Greg, are already a big boy. We should write each other more often so we could learn a lot — especially me, because my English is anything but good. So I hope to receive another letter from you soon.

Last month we had lots of fun here. The children of your uncle Walter were with us and with the boys of your Uncle Gerhard, they made a fine Indian tribe. They went hunting and fishing and inventing the most fantastic stories about their heroic actions. One day Kurt came to me saying, Opa, I killed twenty black widows (a very poisonous spider). The boys had much fun with the burros (donkeys), a species still not extinguished. How nice if you could have been here playing with them; sometime later perhaps.

Greg, are you prepared for school? I suppose the classes are beginning soon. Are you very excited about it? And little Jenny — what about her?

And now, dear Greg, I must come to an end. For your birthday, we wish you all kinds of happiness.

With love, Oma and Opa

Kisses from us to you, Jennie, and your Mom, and Dad.

> ✓+ *Fantastic*
>
> R.D. 4 Box 207-J
> Galloping Hill Road
> Lincoln University, Pa.
> April 9, 1981
>
> Dear Oma and Opa,
> I love you very much. I miss you. I wish I could see you. I am doing fine in school. How are you doing out there? Your dogy is cute. I like it. What is your dogies name? Here is a joke. Why do birds fly south? Give up? Becuse it to far to walk. I am doing fine. So is the rest of the gang. I hope your gang is all right. I like it down there. It's fun down there.
> Love,
> Gregory
>
> We had to practice letter writing at school. We could write to anyone we wanted to so I'm sending it to you.
> Hope you have a Happy Birthday. Greg

Greg's letter

Saturday 9/7/1981: Gerhard and Carol were glad that they were in Dublan so Gerhard could help put out the fire from the alcohol still, before Dad got severely burned. By the time they left to go back to Colonia Juarez, Dad's adrenaline had settled down enough to drive to Nuevo Casas Grandes to get bread.

In September, Dad writes that he hopes that he had not disappointed

Chapter 14   Empty Nesters, 1981 – 1984

Greg with his letter: *Unfortunately I am not very good at inventing and telling great stories. It is curious to observe in myself that the older I get, the more I like children; or is that what they call senility nowadays? Say what you will, but it is so.*

In December 1981 Dad starts having back pain and is now only working in the morning. He writes on 12/6/1981:

My back problems continue and all the doctors indicate that there is no remedy for what they have diagnosed as 'lumbago'. Walter consulted with a doctor in Denver and another in Cd. Juarez. The doctor in Cd. Juarez asked if the pain was constant or not, as if it was constant, it could be cancer. But since this is not the case and confirmed by Dr Salas, it is practically incurable but without danger. X-rays do not show any fractures or anything abnormal, so I have to accept and resign myself to this situation as something incurable. And that is exactly what I am doing! I can attend to business as normal, but have to be very careful of lifting anything or of bending.

Dad wrote to Mary Ann that he had sent 25 liters of vanilla and some canned pineapple through Walter that he hoped we would get at some point. As I was growing up, a vendor would come with a truck full of pineapples and Mom would always buy some and can them. Mom was very frugal and there was never any fruit or vegetable that would go to waste as she canned everything and always had much more canned fruit, jams, etc than we could all eat.

At Christmastime, Walter and family spent their time between Dublan and Colonia Juarez, and when all 16 (Gerhard and Walter and their families) were in Dublan, Mom wrote:

It was very nice, but I was also happy when we were alone again.

1982:

Dad would have as many as ten days when he was feeling really good, then he would have several days where he would be aching everywhere again.

In Germany, Rese was taken to the hospital suddenly and given a pacemaker because she had a very weak heart; Max has cancer of the bladder and has been operated on twice without success. Mom writes that they would like to see both Rese and Max again, but she is not sure if Dad can make the trip, but maybe in the summer he will be feeling well enough to travel. So far no doctor or medication has helped, but Dad still hopes to get to Germany to see his brother for the last time. By late April/early May, Dad is feeling a little better, so they are having some thoughts about going back to Germany. He works every morning and in the afternoon he lies on the sofa until he goes to bed. Their hopes of going back to Germany are becoming less and less realistic.

Mary Ann and I with Greg and Jennie went down to Dublan in August 1982. Shortly after our return Dad writes:

> *It has been two weeks since you all left. Those were very happy days for us two old folks to see all our descendants reunited in complete harmony, with the kids playing and entertaining in grand scale. It is sad that we are all so far apart and that we can't organize something like this every year. Shortly after you left, we had a demand for vanilla as we have never seen before. In 15 days I sold more than I normally sell in 3 months. And the best part is that most of it was sold at the new price after the second devaluation of the peso. Fortunately I had purchased large quantities of material prior to our trip at the old prices, so now the prices are probably double.*

1983:

Antonio Blanco, husband of Maria Blanco and Mom's good friend, dies at age 85. Mom is concerned that her friends are either moving away or dying. She writes:

Chapter 14   Empty Nesters, 1981 – 1984

Ich denke so oft was wird aus mir werden wen ich einmal allein sein sollte da Ich auch keine 20 Jahre mehr bin. Ich wuenschte Gerhard wurde nicht in Col. Juarez leben wenn ich auch nicht viel von Gerhard hatte wen er in Dublan waere, aber die Kinder waren dann mehr hier. Ja ich weis ich sollte keine so dumme Gedanken haben aber eines Tages wird es doch so sein was ich befuerchte.

(Which translates to: I often think what will become of me when I will someday be alone, as I am not 20 years old anymore. I wish Gerhard was not living in Col. Juarez, though I would not see much of Gerhard if he was in Dublan, but the children would then be here much more. Yes I know I should not have such dumb thoughts, but still some day it will be as I fear.)

Dad's back pain is almost all gone but now he gets tired quickly and has a hard time breathing when he walks or exerts himself. He is in the living room each afternoon and only goes and checks on Felipe, his helper, once in a while. Dad continues to have problems getting raw material for his products.

In April it snowed for three days and nights like they had never seen before in Mexico. There was an ice-cold wind blowing for days, with tree branches breaking off the trees and many people losing their roofs or having their autos damaged. Luckily the tin roofs, the installation of which had only now been really tested, held up very well.

Gary (Gerhard and Carol), grandchild number thirteen is born. Mom writes:

Little Gary is very alert and strong — more so than the other six were. He is the second Opa- Opa's head, ears and everything. She ends her letter with: *Seit alle fünf recht herzlich gegrusst von Opa und Oma quien quiere usted mucho, mucho. No me olviden. Mama und Papa.*

Theresa (Rüder and Mary Ann), is born, so now Mom and Dad have

14 grandchildren. Mary Ann and I were at the top limit of the quota set by Mom and Dad's maximum 2 – 3 children. Walter exceeded it by one, but Gerhard and Carol blew past the limit and had as many children as Walter and I put together. I am sure Mom and Dad have forgiven us for adding to the world population. I recall at one of our family reunions Mom would ask Walter who one of the kids was. Walter would always answer: *This one is one of Katherine's*. Katherine has the same number of children that her mother and father did, so the odds were good that Walter's response was correct at that time.

1984:

On 1/9/1984, Gerhard called me to say that Dad was not doing well and that I should come home. I was at the airport getting ready to board a plane when a call came through that Dad had passed away on 1/10/1984. I returned home to gather the rest of my family to take the next available flight. Dad's lungs had finally given out and he went to heaven. The many years of smoking had taken a toll on his lungs to the point where less than 30% of his lungs were still pliable enough to function. He was not quite 85 years old and had worked hard his whole life. I could not have asked for a better Dad. He wrote to me faithfully and was much better at writing than any of his children ever were. He always encouraged us to do our best and sacrificed so that we could go to the better schools to get a good education. He always wanted only the best for us and for each of us to be successful in fulfilling our dreams. Even though we did not always take the paths that he may have wished, he always stood by our decisions. He never gave up on his dream to build a business that he could pass down to one or all of his three sons. I am sure that with Gerhard continuing the vanilla part of the business, it gives him some satisfaction that all his efforts were not in vain.

At his funeral, members of the Latter Day Saints Church sang *To Dream the Impossible Dream* at his gravesite, a song that was selected by Gerhard.

Chapter 14   Empty Nesters, 1981 – 1984

Quicka (far left) with us at Dad's burial.

Chapter 15

Transitory Years, 1985 – 2007

After Dad passed away, Mom spent three to six months every year between Pennsylvania and Colorado, and continued to live by herself in her home for the next 16 years. Her dog, Mitzi, was her companion and always by her side. She enjoyed visits from longtime friends, Licha Gonzalez, Quika Maesse, Natalia Garcia, Gloria Rivas, and Raquel Salais. She also really enjoyed visiting with Lucita Gomez, who lived in Nuevo Casas Grandes, who she knew, along with Raquel Saenz, shortly after arriving in Mexico. The ladies from the Dublan Ward also visited her as they had for many years. By this time, they knew that Mom would not change her religion, so the discussions were non-religious. Her neighbor, Esperanza Saenz, who lived in the house attached to the cheese factory, came to visit often and would let Gerhard and Carol know if something was not right with Mom.

In the summer of 1984, Mom spent three months with us. We took her to the Baltimore aquarium on Sunday, July 1 after which she told us that she had seen enough *pescados* (fish) to last her a lifetime. When we stopped to get dinner on the way back she said that her chicken dinner even tasted like fish.

1985:

Mom writes of one occasion in the spring where a sister of Carmela Wallace invited Mom, Sra Gandara, Chicis Jeffers, and four priests to dinner in Corralitos (the ranch owned by the Wallace's) which was very entertaining, with good food and wine. In that same writing, she happily reports that swallows had finally returned and built a nest on the veranda, where they had previously nested for years before. Apparently the swallows were singing *Las Mananitas* to her every morning.

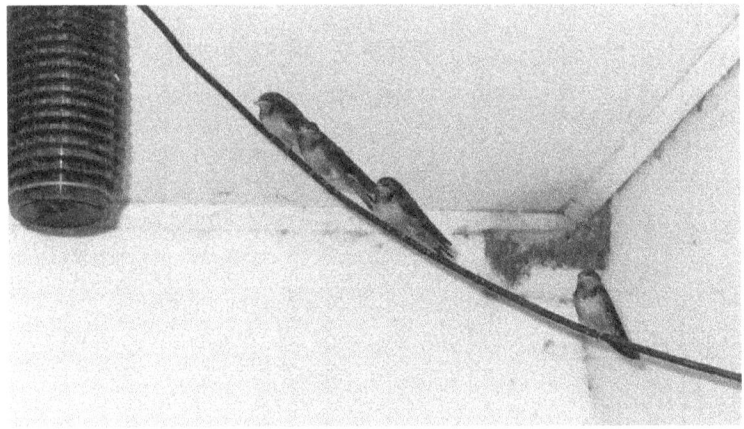

Swallows return to nest in veranda.

We had Oma visit us for a while in the spring of 1985. Our daughter, Theresa, last remembered seeing Oma as she boarded the plane — so every time she saw a plane she said: *Oma?* We were beginning to wonder if she thought that Oma lived on a plane.

During one of Mom's visits to Walter, she wrote that Ann had gone to visit her parents in Wisconsin and Susan and Caryn had gone to a dude ranch outside of Denver, which left Mom alone with Walter, Kurt, and Alan. Mom used to make a great dish, *Bayerische Kraut* and spinach which Walter enjoyed, but which everyone else in his family did not like, so she decided to cook something for Walter that he would normally not get at home.

1987:

Rese, Wolfgang, Helga, and Robert visited us here while Oma was staying with us. Then they traveled on to Denver to visit with Walter, who took them to Mexico so that Rese could finally see where Mom lived. I am not sure what impression Rese had of Mom's surroundings, but she told Wolfgang on their flight back to Germany that now she could die knowing where Ushe had lived all these years.

Chapter 15   Transitory Years, 1985 – 2007

Greg, Tante Rese, Rüder, Jennie, Mom, Mary Ann, Theresa, cousin Wolfgang, and Helga Ertle in our yard.

1988:

As I had a short business trip to Germany I asked Mom if she wanted to go for a few days. She had her suitcase packed in no time and we went for a quick trip to her homeland. She spent most of her time with Rese and her cousin Lena while I worked. She visited her other cousins and we made a quick visit to Winterstettenstadt. By this time Dad's relatives in her age group were all gone, but there were naturally many of their offspring — my many cousins — to visit.

1990:

My wife, Mary Ann, wrote:

We took a big summer vacation by flying to Denver to visit Walter, Ann and kids. We rented a car and drove to Yellowstone National Park for several days, then on to El Paso with short stops to see the Mormon Temple in Salt Lake City, the BYU campus, and several parks in Colorado and New Mexico. In El Paso we crossed the border into Mexico and boarded a bus from Cd. Juarez to N. Casas Grandes, where we spent four days visiting Oma, Gerhard and Carol. The trip was memorable, in that we had the opportunity to see relatives that we hadn't seen in seven years. The bus ride to and from Casas Grandes and Juarez was also memorable, but in a bad way. The ride back to Juarez had live animals on board as well as being overloaded, with people standing in the aisles. The bus still made numerous stops to pick up even more passengers, with occasionally someone getting off. To make matters worse, Theresa had been experiencing a bout of Montezuma's revenge. As was to be expected (but not by us) the lavatory on the bus was not working and could not be used.

Mary Ann to this day refuses to go to Mexico, unless we can drive down.

1991:

Gerhard and Oma went to Germany to meet Katherine, who was being released from her mission in Eastern Germany. This was Gerhard's first trip to Germany and they visited relatives in Munderkingen, Dietershausen, and Winterstettenstadt.

Visit with Mom's families. From Left, Berta, Elfriede (standing), Lena, Freda (Hermann's wife), Fanny, Katherine, Mom, Josefine Schneider (Müller), Hermann Stöhr, Lina Durner (Müller), Rese, and Gerhard.

Visit with Dad's brother's family. From left Wolfgang Ertle, Mom, Max Jr., Rosemarie, Gerhard, Katherine, Senze (Max Sr's wife).

In the mid-1990s, Oma starts having incidents of blacking out while walking her dog, which was of concern to us all. In 1995, while she was with us in Pennsylvania, Dr McLaughlin did a complete physical checkup and ran an ECG and recommended additional tests. At the Southern Chester County Hospital , Dr Maguire, our neighbor, ran the following tests: Stress test, EKG/ECC Echo, EKG/ECC Echo (Doppler), EKG/ECC Echo (Color flow), as well as had her on an EKG/ECC Halter monitor for several days but no issues with her heart were detected. Then in 1998 when she was again visiting us, she had further tests as she was still having her occasional blackouts. All tests indicated that she had some clogging of the arteries that was quite normal for her age. The tests also indicated that she a mild case of cardiac arrhythmia, so she was put on medication to help control this.

1998:

I took Oma to an ENT doctor to check her hearing as she was complaining of not hearing so well. The doctor debrided a large amount of cerumen in her left ear and did a hearing test, followed up with another test in August 1998. In that report the doctor noted:

> *I saw Mrs Schill in follow-up today. Over the course of the last year there has been no significant change in her hearing subjectivity. On today's examination, I removed a considerable amount of wax out of both ears. Again she is noted to have somewhat narrowed ear canals on both sides which is worse on the left than on the right. The audio logical analysis showed some slight worsening of her hearing from the perspective of pure tones. We were able to do speech reception which is somewhat diminished, but we could not do discrimination scores because of a language barrier. Mrs Schill has a sensor neural hearing loss that is symmetrical in nature. It is somewhat worse compared to her hearing test from one year ago. At this point, I think she would certainly benefit from at least one hearing aid having discussed the issues of getting one versus two hearing aids. Given the fact that she is somewhat resistant to them altogether, she would be more likely to use one rather than two. We will set her up for this, and I will see her back in one year for a re-evaluation.*

So Mom got a Siemens hearing aid for her right ear. It helped her when she had it on correctly and turned on. However, this was seldom the case.

In November I had a business trip to Germany so I took Mom with me. We visited some of her relatives over the weekend then I left her with Lena while I worked and came back on the weekend to visit any others that she wanted to see. This was to be her last trip to Germany. We visited her siblings Hermann and Fanny, as well as her other cousins Hermann and Elfriede. All of Dad's siblings had passed away by this time, but she visited some of Max's and Johan's children and their families. By this time Rese had died and Mom said that she did not want to go back to Germany again. Too many of her family and friends were no longer alive and every time she went to Germany she was reminded of just how beautiful it was there, compared to where she had been living and where she had to return to. Her cousin Lena passed away the following year.

Chapter 15   Transitory Years, 1985 – 2007

Top — Lena, Mom, Elfriede, Berta — lower left with Hermann Baur.

2000:

In May, Mom was having more frequent blacking-out spells. The local doctor diagnosed her problem, not as high blood pressure as we suspected, nor a blood clot as Gerhard suspected, but instead her little 'ticker' that kept her heart beating was getting tired and he recommended a pacemaker. Gerhard and Carol decided it was best to take Mom to live with them in Colonia Juarez. Of course Mom fought that suggestion tooth and nail, but Walter and Ann were able to help her decide that going to Colonia Juarez was best for her.

It was shortly after this, in the summer of 2000, that Mom went to stay with Walter and Ann, with an occasional trip to Pennsylvania. It was hard for her to leave her friends as she went around to their homes to say goodbye. She had always complained about the heat and dust in Dublan, but she thought that Denver was hotter than Dublan and enjoyed the air-conditioning at Walter and Ann's. She became the reigning 'puzzle queen' as she would work on up to eight 100 – 150 piece puzzles at a time. As her memory, especially long term, was starting to fail her, she could do the same puzzles over and over again for some time. She enjoyed the challenge of putting them together and the satisfaction of completing one, then taking it all apart again.

There was a park close to Walter and Ann's house where Mom would walk her dog. Ann would usually have breakfast with Mom, discussing the weather and going through the newspaper with her. Walter would be off to work before the ladies got up, but he would come home at noon to have lunch with Mom every day. He would often take her with him to do job estimates and she enjoyed getting out and having Walter's company. Walter would introduce her and try to get her to socialize with any of his German customers while he worked up the estimates. I do not believe Mom ever got a pacemaker. It seemed that with proper diet and medication, her blacking-out spells disappeared. Certainly staying with Walter and Ann instead of living alone made sure that she got regular meals and took her medicine on time.

2001:

On 2/14/2001 while Mom was visiting in Pennsylvania, Dr Belson removed a cataract from her right eye. She got her sight back as a Valentine's gift and was delighted with her new sight. She would say that the TV was now so clear and bright; much better than the TV in Mexico.

In July we had a week-long Schill family reunion at Pacific Beach, Washington. There was Oma with her three sons, 14 grandchildren, and 12 great grandchildren, plus all the spouses — a total of 40 people.

2001 Family Reunion

2002:

During the time that Mom was staying in Denver, Walter succeeded in getting her a Permanent Resident Card (Green Card) on 10/21/2002, as well as signing her up for social security. Now she was a legal resident in both the USA as well as Mexico, while still a German citizen. During this time Mom had a colonoscopy where three polyps were removed just to be on the safe side. Walter told Gerhard that the doctors had taken all her intestines out and laid them on a table — looked at them and then put them back.

2003:

After being in Denver for over three years, Mom started thinking about going back to Mexico, even waking up at 10pm asking when her papers were coming. So Walter decided to take her back to Dublan in January to visit for a few weeks. Mitzi, Mom's dog, had a difficult adjustment as she had to give up the freedom of Walter and Ann's back yard to being tied up all day. Gerhard also had to make sure that Mitzi was fed, as Mom would forget to feed her. However she would not forget Mitzi at night because she would come out of her bedroom at least three times after getting ready to go to bed and remind Gerhard *encarga Mitzi*, (you're in charge of Mitzi).

2004:

In January, Walter sensed an urgency to take Mom back to Mexico. He must've felt something was going on with him and wanted to make sure Mom was taken care of. In late February, Walter was diagnosed with glioblastoma multiforme, a fast growing cancer of the brain. He went to heaven on 6/23/2004, after a tough battle with his cancer.

Walter's Funeral

By this time Mom had lived in her home in Colonia Juarez, in Denver, with several visits to Pennsylvania, and then back in Dublan. These transitions were certainly a little disorienting for her, as they would be for anyone of her age. While she was in Colonia Juarez she thought that she was living in Dietershausen and kept asking for her passport in order to return to Mexico. Gerhard became the primary care giver for Mom in January 2004 and she lived with him and Carol. She still had a few friends left. Licha Gonzalez would often take her for rides which she enjoyed.

Mom's 95th Birthday

2007:

On 6/8/2007, Mom got up during the night and fell in the bathroom, hitting her head above the right eye and bruising her right elbow. A doctor was called who determined that nothing was broken but he told Gerhard to watch for things that might indicate a concussion and to give her a liquid diet. The next day she was alert, but about 7pm Gerhard had trouble understanding her; she complained of a headache and was getting a slight fever. The doctor called an ambulance which took her to the Dublan hospital for a CAT scan. It was determined that blood was collecting on the right side of her brain and needed to be drained. Because of the limited facilities there, they opted to take her mostly unconscious by ambulance to Chihuahua — a 3 hour trip at 120–130km/hr. At the Chihuahua hospital, a 2 hour operation removed a pint of coagulated blood from her head and doctors reported that several veins had ruptured. She was in intensive care hooked up to all the equipment. On Wednesday 6/13, while still in a state of unconsciousness, they decided to gradually take her off the ventilator as she was breathing on her own. Next they were going to try to wake her up, but by the following morning two different doctors believed that Mom was in a coma and only had about 50% brain function. At this point, we decided to take her off all the instrumentation. On 6/15/2007 with Gerhard by her side the whole time, Mom peacefully went to be with her family in heaven. She was a very kind, gentle, softly-spoken person; I never heard her raise her voice to any of us. She went through a big transition in coming to Mexico, staying there for the rest of her life. She certainly was a loyal wife, a dear and loving mother and her cheerful smile is missed. We all admired her courage and strength. To leave her country and move to a foreign country as she did, not knowing the language, the people, or even what her life would be like, and marrying a man that she only knew through correspondence, is truly admirable.

Mom's funeral

Schill gravestones — Dublan Cemetery 2007

Chapter 16

Recollections

Some of my childhood recollections:
Unfortunately there is little documentation about our growing up. In this chapter, I will try to recall some of the highlights, lowlights, and things that still stick in my mind — although those memories are fading rapidly with each passing day.

One of my lasting memories was how Mom always insisted on my wearing a hat when I was to be outside or go anywhere in the sun. I sensed that she was afraid my skin might turn dark and I would lose my German looks. Anyway, I was as strongly opposed to wearing a hat as Mom was insisting that I wear one. I remember one time when I was going out, I went and hid inside a big boiler, a remnant of the lactose factory that was in the fabrica. I could hear Mom and other people calling my name over and over, but I was not about to come out because I knew I would be made to wear that ugly hat. After some time, the calling quietened down and I came out of the boiler. They said that I was all black except for my eyes. Needless to say, not only did I not wear a hat — I also missed out on going to wherever we were supposed to go.

We had a ditch for irrigation that went along the east side of our property line. About every 1 – 2 weeks, water was channeled into this ditch from the man-made lake that the Mormons had built. My brothers and I would play in the ditch, especially after the water was turned off, where we would look for and catch little fish that came in the water and we would have a lot of fun.

My parents usually kept a pig which we would have to feed every day. We would get attached to these pigs, which were obtained as piglets and we cared for them until they were big enough to be slaughtered. When that time came, the butcher, Isidoro, would come early in the morning and get a fire started to heat up some water and salt in a half 50 gallon drum in our back yard. When the time came, we would say our farewells to the pig and we would be told to go into the house. We would usually stand at the window in my parents' bedroom that looked out toward the back yard and even shed a tear or two at times. Then we would hear the squeal and knew that our pet was no more. The butchering took most of the day, as Isidoro would then cut up the pig. The skin with the fat would be cut up into squares and put into the hot water. This was stirred until all the water was gone and the lard had been rendered. We had lots of *chicharones* and lard which was stored in 10-gallon stoneware jars in our parents' bedroom as it was usually cooler than the rest of the house. I remember that for lunch on butchering day we would always have fried potatoes with kidneys which I did enjoy. The cycle would then start all over as we would get another piglet and raise it for the same fate. Some of the things that we would get from the pig were headcheese, pork steaks, and lard for a whole year. (In those days we cooked with lard and even used lard instead of butter when times were hard. It actually was not bad when spread very thinly on bread with a little salt on it.) Dad also used one of the chimneys, a remnant of the lactose factory, to make *rauchfleisch* — smoked meat-like bacon, but mostly meat with very little fat; it was very good. Later on he actually made his own smoker out of two 50 gallon drums with the tops and bottoms of both drums cut out. He welded the drums together to make one long drum and anchored it to the corner between the fabrica and the bodega. The meat was hung at the top and Dad would burn moist sawdust that burned very slowly but made a lot of smoke. After several weeks, the *rauchfleisch* would be ready. We would hang some of these slabs of *rauchfleisch* on the back of the laundry room door and cut pieces off from time to time.

One of our pigs was nicknamed *el venado* (the deer) because he had long legs and was always jumping out of the pen. I remember one morning when we went out to feed him; he was not in his pen as he had jumped out. We searched high and low but could not find him. Then one of us was walking behind the old cheese factory (which had been out of operation for years) and heard an 'oink, oink' coming from somewhere in the back. The cheese factory had several underground tanks about five feet deep, (I am not sure what they were for unless they were large septic tanks for the discarded whey). One of the tanks had no lid and our little pig had fallen in; luckily there was only about four inches of liquid in the tank. The pig was looking up and patiently grunting, waiting for us to get him out. I don't think he jumped out of his pen for some time after that.

El Venado

We always kept a few chickens — one year we had 100 chickens and by the next year we had 200. We would order the chicks and when they were delivered, we would put them in a smaller room that had sawdust on the dirt floor. Chickens are about the dumbest animals that God created. We used infrared lamps to heat the room and when the nights were colder than normal, we would have to go out every couple of hours to check on them and spread them out as they would pile up in a corner fifty high if you let them. Of course the bottom ones were warm — but their survival rate diminished with their position in the pile. The bottom ones could easily be smothered unless we spread them apart. So we had some sleepless nights for a few weeks until the chicks got bigger and tougher. Our classmates would be sleepless because they were out smudging fruit trees. Smudging, creating a smoking fire, was used in those days as a means to raise the temperature slightly in the fruit orchards to keep the fruit blossoms from freezing, as frozen blooms fall off the trees and do not produce any fruit. We had chores to do before and after school. We had to feed and water the chicks and chickens before and after school, gather the eggs and clean out the feeding and watering areas. Once a week we would take the eggs to Nuevo Casas Grandes to sell. According to Gerhard, one of our customers would always put the eggs in a tub of water and if any of the eggs floated, he would reject them. He claimed that if the eggs were not fresh, they would float. Only once did an egg of ours float. Gerhard brought it home and it turned out to be a double-yoked egg. Another nasty chore which we fortunately didn't have to do more that 2 – 3 times a year, was to take out all the now dirty sawdust from the chicken house and replace it with clean sawdust from the lumber mills and carpenter shops in the area.

I remember when I needed to buy a suit for my high school graduation. I had been saving dollars for some time; I would buy them from Dad because he was sometimes paid in dollars for his vanilla. As suits were expensive in Nuevo Casas Grandes and selections were small, Mom decided that I should go to Cd. Juarez on the bus and visit Sra Dienner. (Sra Dienner was the widow of Sr Dienner, an engineer who had come to Casas Grandes with his wife to build the first electric plant in the area. They spoke German and my parents became good friends with them while they were in Casas Grandes. They did not have any children and when Sr Dienner passed away, Sra Dienner went to live in Cd. Juarez.) So Mom and Dad put me on the bus with a live chicken that I was to give to Sra Dienner as a small token of our appreciation. I was not the only one with a chicken on the bus — so the 6 hour bus ride was lots of fun. When I got to Cd. Juarez, Sra Dienner picked me up at the bus station and the look on her face when she saw the chicken was priceless. She asked me what she was supposed to do with a live chicken and I replied that it was for her to cook, but she just shook her head and we put the chicken in her garage. That night she asked me how she was going to cook a live chicken, so I told her I would kill it for her and pluck the feathers. I needed an axe or a big heavy knife but she did not have an axe, so I found what could pass for a machete and somehow was able to cut the head off the chicken. I plucked the feathers, cleaned it and gave it to her to cook. I also cleaned the garage for her; that was one time I wished there had been sawdust on the floor. The next day we took the streetcar to El Paso. We picked out a gray suit that was on sale at Penneys and got back across the border without any incident. I was very proud of my purchase, as close to that time the Mexican peso had devalued from 8.65 pesos to 12.50 pesos to the dollar.

Gerhard was lucky to have a godfather who gave him some nice gifts. He was the only one of us boys who got a BB gun, a Parker ballpoint pen, and a plain red coat — all gifts from his godfather. Santa Claus also brought him a bicycle for not biting his fingernails, but I wonder how Santa kept track of just how long he kept from biting his fingernails, because I am sure if he had kept a good track, he would have taken the bike back. The bicycle became our small pickup as we used it to haul chicken feed (110 # sacks) on the handle bars, which was not easy to maneuver with such a sack over the handle bars. One time I came around a corner by the old Bowman flour mill and ran smack into two horses pulling a wagon. I am not sure who was more scared — the horses or me. How I made it out of there without a scratch and with the bike and chicken feed intact is still a mystery to me, and also how the horses, wagon, and cowboy survived without a catastrophe. The good Lord must've been looking out for all of us.

I remember us shooting one of our chickens with Gerhard's BB gun. How that the chicken dropped over is beyond me — she must've fallen over in shock that one of us actually hit our mark. Well, a dead chicken was a problem. How would we explain to Mom and Dad that we had shot one of our chickens? We figured they would probably never detect one chicken missing since we had so many, so we decided to throw the chicken over the wall between our property and the old cheese factory. We planned to go back there that evening and bury it, but when we went we discovered the chicken clucking away and walking around wondering how it got there. It took us a while but we cornered it and brought it back to be with the rest of the chickens. We never told Mom or Dad about this little incident.

One of our entertainments was building roads and bridges along the front of the house for our two little metal cars that Gerhard and I had.

We even made cars from a block of wood, with four soda bottle caps for the wheels. We also played with marbles; two games we played were 'Ringer' and 'Purga', a variation of 'Poison'. I was never really that good at Ringer as my marbles did not have that much force when I shot them.

I remember coming home from high school one dark night after it had rained. The bus dropped us off two blocks from our house. The first block had a row of trees along one side and a dirt walkway between them and the property that belonged to Taylor's. Once off the bus, my eyes gradually became accustomed to the dark and able to distinguish where the water puddles were; as they were darker than the rest of the ground. I was doing well getting around the puddles — until one of the puddles got up and ran away from me; I don't know who was more scared — me or the puddle. It turned out that there was a black horse laying on the walkway which I had not distinguished from a water puddle. The scared horse proceeded to get up and run in one direction and I ran in the other. Once my heart rate went back to normal and I realized what had happened, I continued on my way home over the railroad tracks.

I remember Gerhard and me challenging our Dad to a race; I don't remember how old we were but we were old enough to think that we could easily beat him. After some prodding, Dad agreed. We would run from the end of our driveway to the railroad tracks — about one block. Gerhard and I were like two dogs with their tails between their legs at the end of the race for Dad easily won. Needless to say I never challenged him again, but Gerhard thought he would challenge him one last time. Gerhard says it was not a challenge — that he ran out of fear. He did something that he was not supposed to do and Dad called him to give him a spanking, so Gerhard decided to run instead. Dad caught him just as he got to the road when a horse-drawn wagon with a family was going by. He spanked him with everyone in the wagon watching, which would not be politically correct today. Being the oldest of the children, poor Gerhard got the worst of the spankings in our house.

In our house in Dublan, only the living room was heated and the bedrooms could get quite cold in wintertime. Mom would ask me to go lie in her bed when it was time for me to go to bed. After I had stopped shivering and was nice and warm tucked under the feather blanket on her bed, she would come and I would then have to go to my own bed and go through the teeth-rattling experience all over again. At the time I thought I was being rewarded by getting to lie in her bed until she went to bed — not realizing that the only reason I was getting that treat was to warm up the bed for my mother.

Rain was not very common where we grew up, but I do recall an occasional good thunderstorm which usually came at night. It was good in the sense that everyone there needed the moisture, but not good if you didn't have a secure roof above you. For some years our roof was not so good and it had a few leaks when we got that rare rain. As Gerhard and I shared a bedroom, if it rained at night we would keep our fingers crossed that we would not hear the sound of the water dripping from the ceiling. If we did hear this dreadful sound, we would try to figure out if it was above us or in the next room. If it was in our bedroom, we would have to get out of bed — something neither of us cherished, and put a bucket to capture the rain that leaked through. If it was over our bed, one of us would be without a bed until the drips stopped; but if it was in another room, we would stay in bed and let Mom or Dad get the bucket.

My mother had a wood stove in the kitchen that she used for cooking, baking, and heating up water for bathing. When my brothers and I were young, Mom would heat up about 5 gallons of water to almost boiling. She had a long, narrow tin tub in which a 4 or 5 year old could lay in and she would pour the hot water in with enough cold water to get the temperature comfortable for bathing. Then she would start with the oldest and give him a bath. When she finished him, she would add a little more hot water (if we were lucky) and bathe the next younger one and so on, until we were all bathed. I could never figure out why the oldest always got to go first as I figured the older ones would be the dirtiest — but Mom saw it the other way around. My brother, Gerhard, seems to think that she started with the youngest first, but that is not the way I remember it. When everyone was bathed, the bath water would be used to mop the floors and whatever water was left would go to water the plants outside. It was so nice when Dad started making distilled water in the fabrica. He would run the water that he used to cool the steam (the steam condensed and became our distilled water) into a large cement bathtub in our bathroom. When he made distilled water, he would distill for a whole day about once a week, so there would be enough hot water for all of us to bathe in a large full tub of hot water. It was filled several times on distillation day, so each of us could have a fresh batch of water. Gerhard recalls that one time he was distilling water until after midnight as he wanted to fill all the containers with distilled water. When he finished, he came in and adjusted the water temperature in the tub to his liking and lay in the tub with the water up to below his nose. He apparently dozed off and had a rude awakening when his nose went underwater.

Cement bathtub. Tub and pipes are original, but tub has been painted.

Mom would bake several large loaves of bread in the oven and when that bread came out of the oven, it was to die for. When the loaves were cool, she would put them into a 10 gallon stoneware container and cover it up. We would eat bread from that baked batch until it was gone; the fresher the bread, the better it tasted, but as we got to the last loaf, it was not as good.

We seldom went to church and it seemed that I did not really belong in any church. I was baptized Catholic and went to Mormon schools, at a great sacrifice to my parents. So I felt like I was straddling the fence between Catholics and Mormons. However my mother did raise us with prayer and she taught us to say a prayer before we went to sleep every night. Gerhard and I have recalled the prayer and translated it:

Bevor Ich mich zur Ruhe lege,
tu ich Händ und Herz zu Gott erhebe
und sage dank für jede Gabe
die ich von Ihm empfangen habe.

This translates to:
Before I lay me down to sleep,
I do hands and heart to God raise
And say thanks for every gift
That I have received from him.

My mother loved to play dominoes. Her friends would come to visit her and they would play dominoes or Chinese checkers. I am not sure if they came to play dominoes or if they came for Dad's cacao liqueur. After my father passed away, she would play with her sons, daughter-in-laws, or grandchildren — anyone up to playing. I noticed that as she got older she became better and better at cheating. She would get her seven tiles and if she didn't like one of them, she would nonchalantly put it back and take another one. It didn't matter if someone saw her doing it or not; if they questioned her, she would plead innocence. When she did not have a tile to play and had to draw tiles, she got into the routine of looking at a tile from the draw pile and if it was not one she could play, she would put it back and draw another one and so on, until she found one she could play.

Gerhard, Rüder, Walter, and Mom playing dominoes in Denver.

Ann Schill's recollections: (daughter-in-law)

It's not so easy to remember back to 1984; that's the year Opa died, Jan 10th. Walter was there for several days with him before he died, as well as Gerhard of course. Walter called me at 4am and I packed up the kids and was on a plane to El Paso by 9am. It was a trying time for us and yet very rewarding to be there with Opa in the bedroom with friends coming to pay their respects. There was much food and visitors, Mexican and Mormon alike; he was beloved by all. Kurt and Susan were especially close to him; Kurt spent three summers, about 2–3 weeks, with them and Susan spent one. When everyone put a shovel of dirt on his grave, Kurt kept shoveling as if he alone would bury him. It was kind of funny and sad.

After that, Oma stayed with us every summer for 3–6 months at a time. Walter went down with trucks full of used stuff for Gerhard in Mexico and filled up the cheese factory. Oma always came back with him, so my kids grew very close to Oma. The last time she was with us for about three years, but Walter took her back in January of 2004 shortly before he got sick. Sometimes I think Walter knew something was wrong with him but not what, and that's why he took her back before he got sick in late February.

We spent Christmases with Oma and Opa and have many fond memories of them. Opa and I used to listen to his taped music of Handel's Messiah, which I sang in my High School Glee Club. Gerhard used to move the furniture in the living room and cram us into the corner, put hot lights on us all and take pictures of all the family. Lol (lots of laughs).

Opa and Oma would go to the Catholic Church with us when we were there. I got the feeling that Opa enjoyed it and had missed it and was glad that I had everyone going. We had many chats about all kinds of things and he always had one of the kids on his lap when he sat down. Walter spent time in the fabrica with him, making vanilla and going through stuff he had brought down for him; Walter was a born 'contrabandista'. Ha ha. We usually went down at least twice a year but later on when the kids got older, only Walter would go and come back with Oma or take her home. During the three years Oma was here, she had a colonoscopy. It was quite interesting; they let me be in there with her and saw everything they saw with their camera. Oma only had a mild sedative and wasn't aware of anything but a little discomfort. She also had cataract surgery on one eye and that so improved her sight. She was thrilled to be seeing all those vapor trails in the sky! We used to sit on a bench in the park and watch them and look at the mountains — as long as I could get her to sit still. After she was gone, people in the neighborhood would ask about her and wonder how she was doing. They had met her, Walter and Mitzi, when they were walking the neighborhood. Walter was always finding German people that he could bring Mom to visit so she could keep up with her German.

Mom on park bench with dog in Denver.

Walter took her over to Calvary Baptist by the house one time. It was a day out for caregivers where they could leave their elderly parents for a few hours and the 'kids' could get a break. When it came time for a rest period, they had everyone in recliners with a blanket covering their legs to rest. (I always had this picture in my mind of pre-scholars lined up and resting on their rugs.) Oma went around handing out blankets; she thought she was there to work! Walter thought she might enjoy time with people her own age but that backfired. She told him in no uncertain terms that she would never go back there again!

Then there was the hearing aid she got at Rüder's. She lost it in our recliner as she always used to take it out. We never did find it; it was one of those great mysteries of the universe! I forgot about the passport thing too. She was always so worried about her passport whenever we went to Mexico and kept opening and shutting her purse looking for it. We finally took it from her and put them all together so she could have some peace of mind; and us too.

Erik grew really close to Oma while she was here those three years. She used to call him her 'love boy'[5]. That's why he was able to give such a wonderful speech about Oma at her funeral. Erik spent a lot of time with us and he was very close to Walter, being first grandchild and all.

Wolfgang Ertle:
(my cousin, son of Rese Kreutle — Mom's half-sister)

Wolfgang told me the following regarding the death of our grandmother:

> *Als Grossmutter am 14 Dezember 1980 starb, habe ich Deine Mutter (Ursula) am naechsten Morgen in Mexico angerufen und ihr mitgeteilt, dass Oma gestorben ist. Darauf sagte Deine Mutter mir, dass Oma sie gerufen habe und zwar genau zu der Zeit, als sie starb. Tante Uschi sagte mir dann noch, sie haette sofort geahnt, dass Oma gestorben sei. Oma starb nachts um 2 Uhr hier in Munderkingen im Krankenhaus und unter Berücksichtigung der Zeitverschiebung rief Oma Deine Mutter genau zur selben Zeit beim Namen. Es gibt vieles zwischen Himmel und Erde, das wir nicht erklaeren koennen.*

(My translation: When grandmother died on December 14, 1980, I called your mother (Ursula) the next morning in Mexico, and told her that her mother had died. Then your mother told me that her mother had called her by name precisely at the time when she died. Aunt Uschi told me then that she immediately guessed that her mother had died. Her mother died in the hospital at 2 o'clock in the morning here in Munderkingen, so taking into account the time difference, our grandmother called Ursula's name at exactly the same time. There are many things between heaven and earth which we cannot explain.)

Wolfgang also wrote the following:

Tante Uschi und Onkel Ali,
Das erste Mal, dass mir noch in Erinnerung ist, besuchten Tante Uschi und Onkel Ali uns in Jahr 1970 zusammen mit Walter. Die beiden Schwestern Rese und Uschi hatten sich viel zu erzählen. Soviel ich weiss, hatten sie sich seit der Auswanderung von Uschi nie mehr gesehen.

Die zwei Schwestern waren vom Wesen her sehr verschieden. Während meine Mutter Rese eher ernst und immer sehr beschäftigt war, nahm Tante Uschi das Leben leichter und war stets heiter-wenigstens wenn sie bei uns zu Besuch war. Onkel Ali sass damals viel vor dem Fernseher und schaute sich Naturfilme an. Er war ganz glücklich, die Filme ohne Unterbrechung anschauen zu Können. Bei uns gab es damals noch keine privaten Fernsehsender und so wurden die Filme nicht durch Werbung unterbrochen. Das zweite Mal kamen die beiden im Jahr 1979 nach Munderkingen. Grosse Ausflüge wollten die beiden nicht machen, sie besuchten lieber die Verwandten und Bekannten. Leider verging die Zeit immer viel zu schnell. Es war das letzte Mal dass sie ihre Mutter, Franziska Stohr, sah.

1987 besuchten wir zusammen mit Walter Tante Uschi in Mexico. Meine Mutter sagte immer, Ich möchte nur einmal sehen, wie und wo Uschi lebt. Als wir dann nach Amerika flogen, ging sie mit uns. Es war ein wunderbares Wiedersehen. Meine Mutter tat damals den Spruch Nun habe ich ja gesehen wo sie lebt, nun kann ich sterben. Nach dem Tod von Onkel Ali kam Uschi mit Rüder im Jahr 1988 wieder nach Munderkingen. Ein letztes Mal war Tante Uschi mit Gerhard im Jahr 1991 zu Besuch bei uns. Gerhard holte damals Kathrine, die ein Jahr in der DDR weilte. Wir sind überzeugt, dass sie nun wieder zusammen sind.

(Aunt Uschi and Uncle Ali,

The first time that I can remember, Aunt Uschi and Uncle Ali, together with Walter, visited us in 1970. The two sisters, Rese and Uschi, had much to tell. As far as I know, they had not seen each other since Uschi immigrated to Mexico. [Note: Wolfgang must have forgotten that Mom and Dad visited there in 1966.] The two sisters were very different by nature. While my mother Rese was rather serious and always very busy, Aunt Uschi took life easier and was always cheerful — at least when she was with us for a visit. Uncle Ali sat in front of the TV a lot, looking at nature films. He was quite happy to watch the movies as at that time, there were no private television stations and so the films were not interrupted by commercials. The two came a second time in 1979 to Munderkingen. They did not want to make any sightseeing trips, but preferred to visit the relatives and acquaintances. Unfortunately, the time went by much too quickly. This was the last time that she saw her mother, Franziska Stöhr.

In 1987, together with Walter, we visited Aunt Uschi in Mexico. My mother always said I just once want to see how and where Uschi lives, so when we flew to America, she went with us. It was a wonderful reunion. My mother then said, 'Well, I've seen where she lives; now I can die'.

In 1988, after the death of Uncle Ali, Uschi came with Rüder to Munderkingen.

In 1991 Aunt Uschi came to visit us with Gerhard. Gerhard came to connect with Katherine, who had spent a year or so in the GDR. [Note: Wolfgang did not mention that Mom and I visited there in 1998.]

We are convinced that they are now all back together.)

Elena Whetten's recollections: (Granddaughter)

My memories of Oma are scattered. I remember going to Dublan from Juarez for the weekend and if I was by myself, Oma would let me sleep in the bed next to hers. If Rosie and I were both there, we would sleep in the middle bedroom. I remember waking up to the smell of her coffee. She would have hers every morning and I couldn't stand that smell first thing in the morning! Oma always took good care of us; she would fix the yummiest food. I loved eating her hamburger patties and potatoes that she would fix in her cast iron skillet and which I have tried to duplicate, unsuccessfully. She would fuss in the kitchen for a long time and we would be ready to eat, then she would wonder aloud where my Dad was and give us a lecture on not coming to eat when you are called. She would also hurry us through the meal and if we lingered, she would tell us that if we ate slowly on an airplane our food would be taken away. I think that must have happened to her once.

She was quite patient with me and I loved to sit with her and put puzzles together. I know I got that love of puzzles from her; she was a master at it, in my opinion! She did ones of all shapes and sizes with the tiniest of pieces. She would also let us join her and her friends when they came to play dominoes with her. I didn't know of any other Grandmas that did that! I loved playing dominoes with her and Quika and learned a lot from her. She would also take us with her to visit Lucita and it always made me feel so grown up.

In the late afternoons we would walk around the block to give her Mitzi some exercise. She always loved her dogs and would frequently say the dog was her only company; I do think she depended on that companionship. In the evenings we would sit and watch the novellas. Sometimes she would read a magazine and pretend she wasn't really watching them, but then the characters would do something and she would comment on it, so we knew she was paying attention. ☺

She always seemed happiest when she had her family around her — despite all the 'complaining' she did. When her sons and their families were gathered at her house for holidays, vacations, or any occasion, she seemed to really come alive and would busily go about seeing that everyone had what they needed to be comfortable and happy.

She was always very supportive of things we did at school and church and would often come to the concerts or plays, activities or programs that we had. I would sometimes get nervous when we had a church activity that we could invite a grandparent to because I worried that she wouldn't feel comfortable. Oma was an example of courage to me on those occasions, because she would participate, despite the language difference and not knowing any of the others very well. I always thought that she was very gracious.

As I got older she would tell me that I was lazy and would never get married. I'm not sure at what point she changed her opinion of me, but I think she was quite pleased when I chose to marry Chris as she found him to be attentive to her. She always seemed happy to see us when we would visit her with grandchildren. She would hold my babies, smile at them and love them. She would observe them, laugh with us, read stories and play with them as they grew. Although she repeated herself a lot near the end and didn't seem to remember many things, I know that she always remembered me and her family. I think she wore out her life in our service and I am so grateful to be her granddaughter and for the heritage that she has left me.

In September of 2002 after I had graduated from BYU, Rosie and I decided to go to Mexico via Colorado because we had understood that Oma's mental capacities were diminishing somewhat. When we got to Walter and Ann's house where Oma was staying, we rang the doorbell and Oma answered the door. We were sad when she didn't really seem to remember us, but she invited us in. She asked where we were from and we responded that we were from Colonia Dublan in Mexico. She told us that she was also from there and said many times that her home was in Mexico. She was working on a simple puzzle which further confirmed to us that her mental capacities were diminished, as we both remember the big puzzles with 1,000s of pieces that she used to do. It was a great visit, however and it was fun to spend time with Walter and Ann (and Kurt).

Rosie, Mom, and Lena in Denver.   *Rosie and Mom doing a puzzle in Denver.*

Mom doing a puzzle in Dublan.

Greg Schill's Recollections: (Grandson)

We didn't make many trips out west, but it sure seemed like we did to me, since most of them happened when I was at very impressionable young ages. The Wild West I had seen on TV came to life for me when I would go to visit my father's family. I can remember running around the walled compound that contained Opa and Oma's house, the fabrica, Aunt Carol and Uncle Gerhard's home, and the cluttered remains of the cheese factory — our personal little isolated oasis in interior Mexico. When people back east heard you went to Mexico, they pictured the pristine beaches and tourist destinations they were familiar with. But I was introduced to something much more special, a world I could never imagine back in the rural farmlands on the east coast; walking to stores to buy candy and soda and fire crackers with US currency that held incredible buying power; setting off firecrackers in red ant hills, with my cousins all scrambling when the wick was lit, but me not knowing any better standing there waiting and watching to see what happened until the ants started swarming at lightning speed after me; helping Opa with my cousins behind the cheese factory moving sulphur-ridden pyrite around in an experiment that I was quite sure intended to convert pyrite into actual gold; sleeping in the bed my father slept in as a child and playing with knick-knacks in Oma's curio that were some of the only real toys my father had as a child; the understanding that I was part of something much bigger than our small family out east when all the family was together. As we grew older, our adventures took us a little further into the rugged countryside with pickup trucks, *charcos* (water puddles on the streets) that took a small army of Mexican children to get through and small firearms aimed at seemingly endless supplies of jackrabbits. Those little pyrite nuggets I brought back to show and share with my friends at home represented a world they would never know or be able to fully imagine. As an adult living in Tucson, I was so thankful to have had the opportunity to make some trips down to Dublan and share that experience with my sons; the little lookout tower cage at the top of a tall skinny rod iron ladder my father had supposedly built with his brothers and the fear in my boys when climbing up that narrow passage just like I had many years before; fresh pecans from the back yard; old Volkswagens you wished could tell their stories; Oma reciting the 'little piggies' on my toddler's toes; the taste of fresh *horchata* (a Mexican beverage); and on my last trip, the feel of the Dublan soil slipping through my fingers as we laid Oma to rest next to my grandfather and an uncle I never knew. I am proud of my heritage and so very thankful that I had the opportunity to experience some of those roots and share them with my family.

Christopher Whetten's Recollections:
(Husband of Granddaughter Elena)

I remember watching world cup soccer with Oma in 2006. We were in Dublan and Spain was playing. Germany was of course the host of that World Cup. She kept saying *oh, cuanta gente*. After I acknowledged her, then she would say *mucho dinero* to which I would of course agree. We continued that exchange for most of the soccer game.

When I first played Chinese checkers with Oma, I played strictly by the rules. I tried to kindly encourage her to play by the rules as well, because I noticed she was making some moves that were outside the norm. When I would remind her that she wasn't supposed to do that last move, she would neither confirm nor deny that she heard me. She would look at me with a look that indicated that it was my turn. After a while I came to the realization that if I couldn't beat her, I would join her. So I started playing Oma's rules, but I still couldn't beat her. So after a while I quit trying to win altogether; I just had to enjoy spending time together and forget about who were the winner and loser.

At the dinner table when I sat across from her I would flare or flex my nostrils at her like a rabbit and she would respond in like manner. After a few moments of us going back and forth, she would finally give up the serious face and we would chuckle as others would complain that they couldn't do that and accuse us of flirting.

Carol and Gerhard brought Oma to Lane's baby blessing (analogous to a Catholic christening) in I believe May of 2006. I always enjoyed joining hands and listening to Oma's memorized prayer in German before eating a meal. Even though I couldn't understand the words, I understood the spirit of it. From the beginning even before I met Oma, I could tell that her grandchildren loved her just by the way they spoke about her. I am sad that I didn't have the opportunity to get to know her earlier in my life, but grateful for the few years that I did have with her.

Rosalynn Renouf's Recollections: (Granddaughter)

One of my more recent memories of Oma was when Jackson and I went down for a visit; it could have been for Mother's Day. Anyway, we were watching an NBA basketball game with Oma and she would ask, *Cuanto questan los boletos?* And we would reply, *Como cien dolares.* To that she would ask, *Cuantas personas van al juego?* We would reply, *Unos cientos.* She would think about it for a minute and then say, *Que buen negocio!* Then after a few minutes she would repeat the same conversation. It is one of the few memories that Jackson has of Oma and I'm glad that he was able to spend a little time with her while she was alive. During that same visit, we spent some time watching *America's Funniest Home Videos* with her. We had a good time laughing at the silly videos.

One of my earliest memories of Oma was when I was maybe between 8 – 10 years old and I was in Dublan with Elena and Gary. Oma made some German pancakes with apples in them. Everybody was saying how good they tasted, but I did not like them. It was all I could do to get them down and keep them down. What I would give to have a bite of one now. I don't remember Oma baking much. In fact the last couple of years I was home, she wasn't eating much and Dad would have to keep telling her that she needed to eat and she would say that she wasn't hungry. I do remember her baking some anise cookies one year and how they had to sit from November to Christmas to get soft. They were delicious. I also remember that she baked a peach pie that I thought was tasty.

One night I stayed overnight with Oma when I was about six or so. I got to stay in the bed next to hers. I don't know why I was there by myself, but I remember my ear hurting in the middle of the night and Oma gave me some medicine. It was the first earache that I remember and the last one. During high school I stayed with Oma one night. She woke up early and made me a nice breakfast and made sure I left to the bus on time.

I will always remember going down to Dublan with Dad on a Friday night. We would get to Oma's and walk Mitzi around the block. I always thought she was mean to Mizti because she never let him take his time and smell everything, but she would very efficiently pull Mitzi around the block for his exercise. I loved going on walks with Oma.

One time I went home from college and Oma was now living with Dad and Mom. I noticed a lump on Mitzi's leg. Dad took him to the vet the next day and the diagnosis came back as cancer, so they had to amputate poor Mitzi's leg. She did her best getting along on three legs after that. Oma went through a lot of 'Mitzi's'. One time she came back from Uncle Walter's and had a new dog; she told us it was 'Terry', but a few hours later she was calling it Mitzi. I remember a couple of funerals for a Mitzi. One funeral that we weren't there for, Mom recorded a little bit of Oma holding and petting Mitzi one last time before he was buried. It was so tender. Even though I thought she was sometimes mean to her dogs, she loved them. She would always tell us that everybody left her, except her dogs. *Ellos son mi company*, she would say.

During the summer when I was little, the men would work in the orchard and it was our job to watch for grape thieves. We would take books and a picnic out there. One time we found some really big leaves that made awesome umbrellas so we took them to show everybody. Oma was so mad at us for cutting off the rhubarb; I think she ended up cooking something with it that day. I don't remember seeing Oma mad very many times, but I will never forget that one.

Oma didn't really talk about Opa that much, but she would always bring up how punctual he was when my Dad was running late for lunch. She would say that he always had breakfast at the same time and lunch was always at 12; he was never late. Oma would always whip us up a good meal when we would go visit her. I loved her potatoes and hamburger.

Oma loved when she had family visit. She would light up when her children or grandchildren came from the US; she would laugh with them and her eyes would sparkle. Oma would come up to Colonia Juarez or we would go down there for Thanksgiving dinner. I loved eating on Oma's nice dishes at her house. She would make her special salad with apples.

Oma had a cute little Christmas tree that she would put up in the corner of her house. She had the coolest Christmas decorations, especially the little bird in the ball and the icicles. She always had treats for us. I don't know where she got them, but she would always give us some chocolate or gummy bears when we would come over. Sometimes she would try to give us money when we helped her with something. We would always say no and she would try to put it in our pockets. She was always so kind.

I miss playing dominoes with Oma. On rare occasions we would go into her house and she would have a guest over and they would play dominoes together. I would make an awkward exit as quickly as I could. Sometimes I would get to take a bath in Oma's tub as I loved how high her tub was and using her zest soap. I would sit in her bathroom and smell her lotions in her cabinet; I was intrigued by everything she had.

Some weekends we would get to her house when it was dark outside and she would be watching her novellas. She would catch us up on what was going on with them. We would wait for Dad to finish up his tasks so we could go back to Colonia Juarez on Saturday nights and sometimes we would wait at Oma's house. We would fall asleep because Dad always took longer then he said he would and she would cover us up with blankets.

I loved when Dad would bring Oma up for our performances or graduation, etc. I didn't fully appreciate it then, but it felt complete when she was there. She would always look her best when she came up. I loved Oma's hair — she would always put it up with bobby pins. She always smelled of laundry soap.

After Oma got back from a trip to Uncle Rüder's, she would always tell us when we ate that we needed to hurry and eat because the airline people would come and take away the food if you didn't.

Oma would always tell us the story of when the boys went to church and she asked them what they learned. Uncle Albert said, *Pan agua y sit down.* He received bread and water and he obviously got up and out of his seat a couple of times and must have been told to sit down.

I love the story of when we were at the reunion in Washington and Oma would see kids running around and she would ask who's kids they were and Uncle Walter would tell her Katherine's.

Gary Schill's Recollections: (Grandson)

Memories of Opa:

I don't have any memories of Opa, but the sense I got when I would meet someone who knew Opa (often one of my dad's friends or acquaintances) whether it was in Nuevo Casas Grandes or home in Dublan, was that he was a person with integrity, well-respected in the community, smart and a hard worker. I can see for myself that he was resourceful and had many ideas of things he wanted to create (and often was successful). He must have mastered the art of writing and was able to communicate well, considering Oma chose to leave Germany to be with him.

Memories of Oma:

Some of these come from pictures that have jogged a distant memory and others I remember like they were yesterday.

I must have been about 6 or 7 when we had a church activity one Saturday to which grandparents were invited. I have a picture with Oma, Elena, Rosie, and me. I was happy Oma was there and had come up from Dublan to be there for us. She would also come to some Christmas programs, school plays, band concerts, school graduations and it was always fun to see her there. I also have a vague memory of her coming to watch a basketball game when we played a tournament in the Dublan gym. It was fun to see her there and I appreciated her interest in me.

On numerous occasions Dad would take us down to Dublan on Friday evenings, (if he needed to water or make vanilla). Before Oma went up to stay in the U.S. and was still very healthy, we would often stay at her home. I have many memories of watching tele-novelas with her on Friday evenings before going to bed. Her house was warm and we would be watching a show and she would laugh and say things like *que tonterias*, which would make me laugh. Sometimes we would be waiting for my dad to finish up Saturday evenings and there were a few English channels that Oma received. I remember several Walker Texas Ranger episodes where Oma would say 'wuhouuu' like she often did. At times I would be watching TV with my mouth open and she would catch my attention and say *con la boca cerrada no entran las moscas*. We never had a hard time communicating, she in her 'Spanglish' with a German word thrown in every now and then, and me still learning Spanish ... but we got along great.

Speaking of things she said, I remember she would often be working around here and we would hear her humming. I'm not certain, but I think most of us thought she was humming to the rhythm of the washing machine. Sometimes she would tease me for always wearing a hat. I loved my hats and she got a kick out of the fact that one was always on my head.

Some of my favorite memories are waking up in her house and having *Choco Krisps,* or another name-brand cereal, that she often had at her house. She also had a kind of Bimbo sweet roll that my dad often brought her and which she always shared with me for breakfast. But the food I enjoyed the most was her lunches. Saturday around noon, when my dad and I (or siblings) were in Dublan, without fail, she would cook lunch for us. It was usually a hamburger-type meat patty with potatoes. To this day I have not yet been able to replicate those potatoes; she cooked and salted them perfectly. I think it was after she returned from visiting you and Uncle Walter and she still wasn't living with my parents that she wasn't eating. So my dad started ordering food to be delivered to her three times a week. By this time on Saturdays she had stopped cooking lunches and would offer the leftovers which were good. I think this was how my dad and mom discovered that she had stopped eating during the work week, because as time passed there were more and more leftovers. That is when they decided she needed to live with us, (my memory as to the timeline is a little hazy there but I think that's kind of what happened).

One more thing about her food, I remember she always had a glass candy jar that regularly contained *Hershey Kisses*. Often they were just the plain silver-wrapped ones, but every now and then she had ones with white chocolate or almond-covered or mint chocolates. She always made sure the jar had something in it when we were there. I think Uncle Walter would bring packages of candies when he would come down to visit. She never showed me where her stash was, but she seemed to ration them out well, so we always got a treat when we visited her.

I often have memories of her with Mitzi. We all know she loved Mitzi(s) but some of the fondest memories I have was when we would come down and Mitzi would go crazy and run around the house. It made Oma laugh and she really enjoyed watching Mitzi go crazy. She also invited Mitzi to watch TV with us and would let her sit on the couch, which you could tell Mitzi ate that up. I remember Oma giving Mitzi baths and walking her around the block every evening. If we were around she would invite us to walk with her and she would let us hold Mitzi's chain which was always fun.

I remember every now and then I would walk into her home and she would have someone from the community over. Sometimes it was a casual visit from ladies in the Dublan ward, which I appreciated seeing because they were showing an interest in her. I also liked seeing her interact with friends. Oma showed a genuine interest in her friends. I always thought she was very proud of me when I would come into her home or dad and I were picking her up from her friend's house and her friend would gush about how grown-up we were getting or how big we were. I think she shared in that gushing, (mostly by her friend, but I think it made Oma happy).

I remember one time when my grandpa Packham was visiting and she was so warm with him. They were very kind to each other and I loved seeing that.

I have one memory of when Alan and Caryn were visiting and I was driving the tractor like we would sometimes do. I don't think I realized that I wasn't sharing like I should have and she kind of scolded me for it (for good reason) and she told me I needed to let them drive. She was so happy to have them visit and wanted it to be the best experience for them.

I remember she was so good at showing her appreciation. Saturdays when we would go down to help my dad, we were often asked to take care of Oma's yard. I loved doing that because (1) it wasn't as overwhelming as taking care of the entire property, (2) cutting Oma's grass in her yard was a piece of cake compared to the ditches and other grassy property we had to take care of, and (3) she would often come out as I was finishing the task at hand and slip me $1, $2, $3 or some amount in pesos. She would say how beautiful it was and when I said I really couldn't take it, (although I really wanted the money), she would insist and I wouldn't argue. I think she knew that was something special to me and she made an effort to go out of her way and express her gratitude. When the grass was cut, the sticks/leaves picked up, or hedge trimmed, she would often let Mitzi run around without his chain and that was always a good feeling. Mitzi would also be let off his outdoor chain when we arrived (and she would go crazy outdoors just like she would indoors), which always made Oma laugh.

On several occasions I remember either Uncle Rüder or Uncle Walter calling her each Saturday. It was a good example and a lesson for me to regularly connect with your parents, but I saw how much she appreciated talking to you guys. And of course as the telephone lines weren't always reliable or her hearing started to get fuzzy, I could tell that she got frustrated knowing there was a desire to talk but she wasn't able to.

I guess my final memory is seeing Oma interact with my dad, Uncle Rüder, and Uncle Walter. Those times were always so fun, as everyone tended to be able to dish out a little teasing, (the ring leader of course was probably Uncle Walter) and to see Oma's sense of humor and to see her laugh at the jokes and *tonterias* were really fun times to watch and experience.

Theresa Reed's Recollections: (Granddaughter)

I always felt so grateful to have the opportunity to spend several weeks in the summer with Oma visiting us in Pennsylvania. From hours of dominoes; (Lord knows she loved her dominoes — I played more dominoes in those summers than in my entire life), to her Perry Mason TV dates, I have some great memories of Oma.

I can remember having multiple German love novels laying around for Oma to read and I believe she would often read them more than once. I always imagined what all those stories must have been about, but I know Oma loved reading them. I also remember her first time wearing a swim suit and how Mom and I convinced her to take a dip in the pool. She kept repeating over and over that it was crazy and that we were crazy, but she smiled the entire time and loved that pool adventure! I know my Dad didn't believe us when we had Oma call him from the pool to tell him she was swimming. We had to snag a photo to document the occasion.

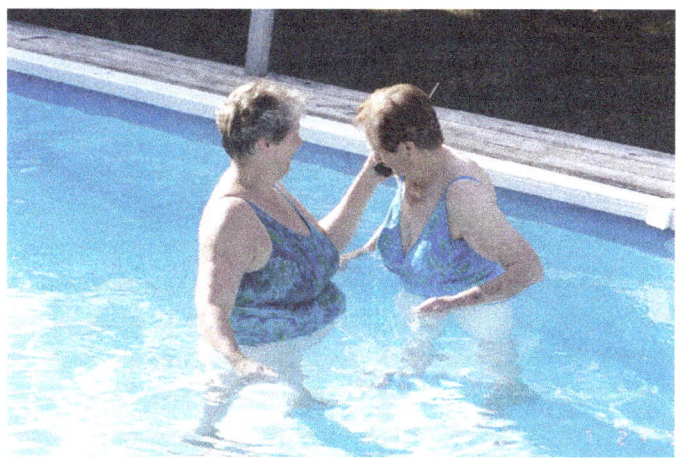

Mary Ann and Mom calling me to tell me that Mom was in a swimming suit.

I also remember Oma's love for dogs, (well all animals, but definitely dogs). She was always so happy with our little Chelsea and wanted her to sit with her on the couch, cuddling. Chelsea adored Oma and was her best friend during those times. Oma's heart was so big, especially for her grandchildren and animals! We also rescued neighborhood stray cats and Oma enjoyed playing with the kittens. I used to give Oma manicures and paint her nails once a week or every couple weeks when she was with us. She always loved this pampering time and it was a great way to bond with her.

Theresa doing Mom's nails.

I didn't speak Spanish or German, but somehow I always felt very connected and close to Oma. She always tried so hard with her English and I would attempt my broken Spanish — yet you could always walk away from spending time with Oma with a smile on your face and renewed.

Oma was always up for anything! I don't think I ever heard her complain and always faced every adventure with a smile. I too remember her constant humming and it is something I still hear when I close my eyes and think of her.

I also remember visits to Mexico, (they were so few and I wish we had so many more), but Oma took such pride in her house and her friends. Watching her laugh with others is something that sticks out in my mind of days in Mexico.

Susan Griffin's Recollections: (Granddaughter)

I have very few memories of Opa; most of them are from family pictures. Many of my memories of Oma include my Dad — which often reminds me of how much I miss them both. I worked most Saturdays with my dad (which is my own special memory of him). My dad would always make the time to call his mother on Saturdays, usually after we closed or when we were slow. I remember the frustration of the phones not always being reliable and he would try and try until he was able to get through; him calling and talking to his mother is one of my favorite memories of my dad.

One of my favorite memories of my dad and Oma is when we were young and would go to Mexico. We always stopped in Deming and somehow managed to fit more 'stuff' into the cars. For those that remember Walter's caravans, it was quite a sight. But he always stopped at the grocery store and stocked up on food for her freezer and for her closet — specifically Hershey kisses and chocolates. Then we would hit Kentucky Fried Chicken and buy a couple buckets for her. She loved her KFC!

I remember sitting at her kitchen table in the morning while my parents were still sleeping, and she would have all the cereals and milk out for us. I loved reading the back of the boxes — I couldn't understand the language, but the games were the same, while she milled around the kitchen making her coffee and eating her sweetbread. To this day a box of *Fruti Lupis* will invoke a memory. What I remember most about her is when she spent so much time with us as she got older. She was there when Erik was very young and loved him deeply. She always called him her 'love boy' and I am pretty sure that she would sneak him half her food at lunch when we would feed them. Often my dad or I would go home at lunchtime to eat with her when my mom was traveling or working. I would tell her I was hungry and that she should eat with me, so she would try to fix me a plate and go back to watching TV. Ha ha — she knew my tricks, but then I would invite her to eat with me and pout and say, *please I don't want to eat alone*, and eventually she would eat something.

Her love of animals was great. While watching western movies when the *caballeros* would get shot off their horses she wouldn't say a word, but oh boy if the horse got shot or fell down, she would gasp and say *poor horse*. She would tell my kids about how much she loved KFC and she would tell them *the States has better chicken than Mexico* and while she took another bite, say *poor chicken*. To this day when we have chicken, someone usually says *poor chicken* and we all laugh.

Erik and Georgia both learned to count and recognize patterns with Oma — dominoes; they both started playing with her at a very young age. They loved sitting there playing dominoes and spending time with her. Often they would do puzzles with her, all the little animals — the fuzzy bunnies and ducklings that would come alive with each piece. As they got older we would play Chinese checkers too. Oma was good, but you had to watch her because those marbles just magically made their way across the board and then before you knew it, she had won! She hated losing and would play until she won or won enough and then be done. I am smiling as I recall her 'sore loser' face and my dad teasing her about it.

As she got older her German 'Spanglish' became harder to understand, but what was never hard to understand was how much she loved her family; her boys; her grandchildren; her life. I will forever miss and also treasure holding her hand as we sat next to each other. A family of hand holders — which may sound strange — but for me it means more than anything. She was a strong, resilient, loving and kind woman. I feel truly blessed that I got to know Oma as an adult, and that my children knew Oma and that she was a special part of their lives as well.

Katherine Bess's Recollections: (Granddaughter)

I loved the fact that Oma and Opa lived next door to us, so I saw them on a daily basis until we moved to Colonia Juarez when I was 12 or 13.

Opa taught me, by his actions, what the word polyglot (knows multiple languages) meant. He was SO amazingly intelligent. When I was in high school, I used to look forward to going down on Saturdays and have him tell me what my Social Studies vocabulary words were, because he was faster than any dictionary. It always blew me away that he knew Spanish to that depth. He once told me he knew several other languages too … like French. He often referred to Casas Grandes as Casas Chuecas (crooked or bent houses). I was never sure if he was referring to the architecture or the corruption. Ha ha.

I loved learning words in German from them. I could understand quite a bit, but since we mostly spoke Spanish back, my vocabulary was limited to household objects and everyday occurrences. After Opa died, Oma spoke a lot less German, and her Spanish became her own unique language.

Opa:

Working outside in his gold pile … telling me about his plans to make paint.

Working in his shop … letting me help him bottle vanilla or lotion. Laughing at me when I took a great big whiff of some eucalyptus mixture; it burned going down my airway!

Getting so angry about the news … especially as we started with hyperinflation. He used to always say if he were a Mexican, he would go to Mexico City and shoot the president.

Water distilling Saturdays meant there was lots of hot water, so we could take a bath in Oma and Opa's big tub. Since at my house we only had showers, this was a fun treat.

Opa calling her *Maisle*; it was a term of endearment — means little mouse. It wasn't until I was in Germany that I learned it was spelled *Mauslein*.

Resting in his reclining chair … especially towards the end. I was 15 when he died, and his death was life-altering for me, because it was the first time I had ever encountered a death that affected me personally. It forced me to pray to gain a sure knowledge that I would see my Opa again after this life. Up until that point, it was just something cool I heard about at church, but didn't really think about whether or not it was real. The knowledge I gained at that time, helped me immensely when Uncle Walter died, when Oma died and when my baby (Xander) was stillborn at 38 weeks. It made the pain of loss just a little less raw.

Opa in his coffin in his bedroom with the window open in January. I loved that none of it was clinical.

At his funeral in the Catholic Church by their house, there was a very old woman with very baggy gray tights passing around the collection plate. I held my breath the whole time, hoping she didn't die right then; she was so old.

Oma and Opa:
Domino Sundays, where Quika and Senora Gandara would come over and play dominoes for hours.

Oma and Opa going to Casas … Oma would hold onto the grab-bar over the door of the Volkswagen any time Opa drove. Good thing she never drove with any of my teenagers!

Going to Chihuahua with one or the other of them for my braces. Opa went with me several times, and so did Oma … until she fainted one time in the hot sun. That was scary for me; I kept thinking about having to call my dad to tell him what happened. Thankfully she recovered and we got home safely.

Oma calling Opa … Ali komm zum essen. At least that is how I remember her saying it.

Oma's cooking:
The *codos* (elbow macaroni) sautéed in oil until browned … with Maggi in a very odd mushroom-shaped pan. I still can't make them the way she did.

The anise cookies that took *forever* to soften, so we could eat them. Seriously, she made them right after Thanksgiving so they would be 'done' by Christmas.

Making sauerkraut every fall.

The one and only time we tried making tamales.

Being introduced to *cesos* (brain), *riñones* (kidneys) and *leberwurst* at their house. We ate heart, liver and tongue at my parents' house, so it wasn't that far of a reach, I guess. None of my kids have tried any of those.

Thanksgiving and Christmas dinner with as many Schills as could make it. Man, those were fun.

Oma and I spent a lot of time together, especially after Opa died. She would always scold me for not being 'proper' when I wore my jeans into Casas to see the dentist, etc.

We flew to Denver to stay at Uncle Walter's for a couple of weeks at Easter before I went out to work there my first summer away from home. I loved watching how much Uncle Walter loved his mom, and how well he treated her. He always was looking for ways to show her how much he loved her … bringing her treats, going on walks, laughing about his new sprinkling system that Mitzi had installed, (the dog had put holes up and down a hose in the back yard).

Some of her sayings that I still remember fondly (with her meanings) are:

El es mas loco que un chivo (he is crazier than a goat)

Kety, komm zu Bett (Katherine, it is bedtime) … *Kety, komm an* (Katherine, now.)

I had spent a couple of weeks at Uncle Walter's right before I went to Germany on my mission. He told me a lot of things about Oma and her life before she came to Mexico. I was really grateful for that because when I told her I was going to go on a mission, she told me that *the train was going to leave the station* and I would be so old when I got back (23 years old) that nobody would want to marry me. Ha ha. I remember Uncle Walter saying she was 28 when she got married; it was fun to hear her reaction when I called her out on the age factoid.

Towards the end of my mission, Uncle Rüder and Oma were going to come pick me up. My Mission President said one of my parents had to be there if they wanted to pick me up. I am SO very grateful my dad decided to go, (or they took him, depending on who is telling the story). We got to tour the relatives, see Oma's house when growing up, see the streets where she was known as the *Dorfbesen* (town broom), the town where Opa was raised, some of Opa's family graves … It was one of the highlights of my life, to be there and see some of the things Oma had told me about all my life and to hear her talk Spanish to the German relatives and German to my dad.

I loved coming back home between semesters in college and hanging out with Oma again ... then Ted and I came down and introduced her to our future spouses. I was glad Eric could communicate with her somewhat. She came up to Col Juarez with everyone for Ted's and my double reception. A couple of years later, Eric and I came home for Christmas and brought our calico cat, Patches. I don't know if she had ever seen a calico cat. She found Patches' coloring quite amusing. The next time Eric and I went to Mexico, we brought Breton with us and it was fun to watch her interact with my baby. We have pictures of her visiting us in Vancouver Washington, which was also fun. I loved watching her see how green it was there ... it must have brought back memories of Germany. Going back to Casas after having lived in Germany, only served to emphasize how very different the two places were. She was an incredibly strong woman in every sense of the word. I called her every once in a while after that, but it was hard ... the connection was bad and as her memory got worse, she would ask me every time I talked to her when I was going to come and visit her. We were both crying every time I hung up. I was glad I got to go home as many times as I did.

I am also grateful I got to go to Oma's funeral and participate in the Mass by doing a reading. I wanted so very badly to participate somehow, as a tribute to one of the finest women I have ever had the pleasure of knowing. I was also happy Uncle Rüder gave my parents' permission to do Oma's temple work, and Courtney and I had the honor of completing that for her. She did many things for me as I was growing up, these were small things I could do.

One of their biggest legacies is while they may not have had much in the way of money, they were very wealthy in things that really matter long term, shaping future generations ... raising their boys, with the work ethic they had, and the way they would do anything for each other, is something I hope carries through to my own children.

I *cannot* wait to see either of them again. The older I get, the more excited I am to be able to be reunited with them some day and 'hang out' with them like I used to.

Jennie Schill's Recollections: (Granddaughter)

I have an unfortunate limited memory, but here are some of my memories of Oma. (I don't really remember Opa at all — except for the picture of him and me on our back deck; he's dressed all nice and I'm wearing a Superwoman t-shirt.)

Greg, Opa, and Jennie on our deck — ca 1982.

It's because of Oma that I wanted so badly to learn to speak Spanish; I wanted to be able to talk to, and know, my grandmother. I was shy about trying out my limited grasp of the language, but between her limited English and great Spanish and my lousy Spanish and great English, we were able to carry on some basic conversations and laugh. And it didn't matter that we were never able to get very deep in a discussion without my dad's help, because we had dominoes and dogs. Oma was a domino's shark, and she could go for games on end without tiring — probably because she usually won. And oh, how she loved dogs (as did I) including ours, which had the same name (Mutzeh) as every dog I think Oma ever had. She used to slip our Mutzeh scraps of meat and other pieces of food under the table, trying to time it when my mom wasn't looking. And that grin when she was caught … priceless.

I remember visiting Oma in Mexico and appreciating how simply she lived. Seeing some special, foreign foods she cooked (and knowing how picky I was at that age, I probably missed out on enjoying). Eating some amazing German foods, like *spätzle*, that I probably never would've known had it not been for her — and that, lucky for me, my mom started cooking. Feeling like I'd stepped inside a mystery book, yet arrived home, when my dad would take us exploring through Opa's old fabrica. (How I wish I could have known Opa.)

I'm still dreadfully far from mastering Spanish and although I've lost the greatest benefit, I still love visiting foreign lands where I can dabble in it. And whenever I do, I think of Oma and how she was my inspiration, probably without her even knowing it; and I'm grateful. I feel so lucky for the times I got to spend with her. You really don't need words to feel love.

Mary Ann Schill's Recollections: (daughter-in-law)

Opa:
My first memory is of the visit in 1972. I am not sure that I recall why he did this ... but, I remember that he gave a rose to a neighbor in the carriage house where Rüder was living (and which became our first home together). I saw that, although he was a quiet man of few words, he had a thoughtful, romantic side to his nature. I vaguely remember that the dinner at my parents' house was on Mother's Day. So perhaps, that was why he presented her with the 'token' rose. I recall our motor home trip from Denver to Mexico. He was a trooper, riding 'shotgun' the entire trip. I assume he was helping to navigate, as I was not (nor am I yet) a good navigator. Our visits to Mexico were not very often and, looking back, I wish we had spent more time visiting them, so that I could have gotten to know him better. Sadly, I believe that I felt a great deal of apprehension to try to communicate due to my inability to cross the language barrier. The Opa that I remember was always kind, thoughtful, and caring.

Oma:
Oma always seemed to have a zest for life. I don't ever recall her being unkind, angry or unappreciative. She always loved freely, not expecting

anything in return. I, too, recall her adventurous side ... willing to wear shorts while visiting us during the summer, putting on her first bathing suit and taking a dip in the pool. I highly doubt that she would have done it if her son would have been there, as I don't think she would have allowed any male to see her 'half naked'. I recall a couple of car rides where she would duck if we passed under a tree with a branch hanging low or shield herself if we drove through water that splashed onto the windshield. I loved that she was willing to share her food dishes with me, teaching me how to make her creamed cauliflower or making fresh potato chips for all of us when we would visit her. Playing dominoes with her was always an experience, (as many of us can attest to). She loved her *Hawaii Five-O* and *Murder She Wrote*, her German love stories. I will never forget the reaction she had to tasting her first *Sour Patch Kid* ... I wish I had a video because it was priceless! She loved the simple things in life — family, friends and pets ... we were all blessed to have her be a part of our lives.

Mom in shorts on dock on the Bohemia River.

Endnotes

1. Swabian (Schwäbisch) is one of the Alemannic dialects of High German. It is spoken in Swabia, a region which covers much of Germany's southwestern state Baden-Württemberg, including its capital Stuttgart, as well as the rural area known as the Swabian Alb, and parts of southwestern Bavaria (Bavarian Swabia). Ursula and Alois were born in this region.
2. Mrs Maria Hardy received a Doctor of Obstetrics degree in Utah and began delivering babies in 1912 in the Mormon Colonies in Mexico. After a move to Arizona in the mid-1910s, she returned to Mexico in 1922 and began delivering babies again. She lovingly delivered over 1,000 babies. My siblings and I were among those she delivered.
3. Mrs Wagner, Clara Mathilda Walser Wagner, and Ursula soon became good friends. Mathilda (Tilly) and her husband, Albert Christian Wagner, were about the only other persons, other than Alois, that spoke German. Albert was a carpenter who had come to Mexico to help build the railroad coming from Cd. Juarez to Nuevo Casas Grandes and which connected to the sawmill center of Pearson (now Mata Ortiz). I remember that after Tilly's husband died and she was having difficulty getting around, my mother would go to her house a couple of times a week to help her with bathing and other chores. I know that Tilly was always trying to convert my mother to her religion. She had been successful in converting her husband and would have liked to see our whole family converted as well. If my mother would ask her a tough question or ask why something Tilly said was the way Tilly described it, Tilly would always answer, well, *dass ist mal so* (well, *that is the way it is*).
4. *Comadre* means Godmother in Spanish.
5. Mom would tell Erik, Susan's son, *yo luv you* (I love you). This expression struck a chord with Gerhard, Ann, and myself and we frequently use it when we e-mail or talk on the phone.

Appendix 1

In September 2004, my cousin Hermann Baur published his memoirs *Wie es damals war*, which translates to *How it was then*. When I visited him in 2005, he gave me a copy to give to Mom. He wrote the following on the inside cover.

Viele Grüße an Usche

This translates, Many greetings to Usche.

He wrote the following on page 29:

> Nicht vergessen soll Usche sein, die ledige Tochter von unserer Gotte – unsere Cousine. Sie wurde von uns aber geliebt wie die ältere Schwester. Diese war in der Obhut der Großmutter und nach deren Tod gehörte sie in unsere Familie. Großvater, so wird erzählt, hat das Mädchen als lediges Kind missachtet. Usche lebt heute mit 94 Jahren in den U.S.A. bei ihren Söhnen. Im Jahre 1936 hat sie einen großen Schritt gewagt und ist damals mit dem Schiff nach Mexiko und hat dort noch auf dem Wasser ihren Brieffreund geheiratet. Diesen Schritt hat sie nie bereut und hatte danach drei wohlgeratene Söhne.

My translation follows:

Not to be forgotten is Usche, our cousin, the single daughter of our aunt. She was loved by us like our oldest sister. She was in the care of our grandmother and after her death she belonged in our family. Grandfather, so it was said, neglected her as a single child. In 1936, she ventured a huge step and left on a ship to Mexico and while still on the water married her pen pal. She has never regretted that step and had three sons. Today, at 94 years of age, Usche lives in the USA with her sons.

My interpretation of 'single' here is 'out of wedlock'. Apparently Mom's grandfather was not too pleased that our grandmother had Mom out of wedlock.

Appendix 2

All I ever got my mother to write about herself was written on the two pages following my translation.

As a little girl I went to school as all the other children with my satchel full of apples since I never ate breakfast. When I got out of school, I went to Blaufeld (a restaurant, brewery, and garden cafe) where high society people came. I left after 1 ½ years because of overseer never left me alone and constantly ridiculed me. He was over 60, a bachelor, and sick. Then I went home for some time because I was bored. I then responded to a help-wanted ad and went to work for Uncle Mile. I stayed with him until I went to Mexico. From him I learned a lot. I helped him wherever I could — in his office and going into the forest to look for insects. He had a very large insect collection. He was like a father to me. We were one and all. I should have stayed with him and not gone to Mexico, as his wife was a Jew and had to go. He never heard anything from her again; certainly they gassed her. So he was left alone. He had no children. He wanted none from a Jew. He always wrote to me when I was in Mexico. Ali wrote to him often too. When I was in Germany, we visited his grave and laid flowers on it. I cried a lot. Maria, his only sister, told me that he always talked about me. He had also written to Mr Weppen in Chihuahua who knew Ali. He was the German Consul in Chihuahua. Mr Weppen shared all good things about your father. He was also a pharmacist and knew Ali very well. So I went to Mexico; first to Hamburg. Uncle Mile took me to an inn de Hapak (ship company). I stayed there with many other passengers until the ship departed (Iberia). There I was taken under the wing of the Head Steward. He was a nice old man. Since I was the youngest and traveled alone, I was his favorite and he spoiled me. Once I was in the music room where I had left a book that I had started reading. When I opened the book again, there was a note which he had left that read, 'Mountain flower wrongly situated, Ursula goes to Mexico where her sweetheart ordered her'. The Captain gave me a white and blue ribbon in memory of my first Iberia voyage.

Appendix 3

List of products/services that Alois made/sold/used (in alphabetical order):

- Alcohol (Pure Ethanol from denatured alcohol)
- Analytical testing of Barite
- Battery solution
- Bismuto (Pepto Bismol) had to be kept refrigerated because it didn't have a preservative.
- Bordeaux mixture for tree grafts. (He made his own soap which was required to make this.)
- Bread
- Brilliantine (lavender)
- Bronze casting (rods)
- Cacao Liquor (Never sold — only for private use)
- Cloralex (Clorox)
- Coffee Liqueur (Never sold — only for private use)
- Consulting on getting sap out of trees
- DDT (Liquid Fly Spray)
- Deodorant (liquid for bathrooms)
- Detergente 'REX' (in Gómez Palacio, Durango)
- Distilled water
- Dr Hatch salve for lesions. (People are still asking Gerhard for it.)
- Embalming fluid
- Furniture polish
- Grease for wagon wheels
- Hair lacquer
- Hand lotion
- Hydrochloric Acid (HCl)
- Hydrogen gas
- Iron Oxides (pigments) from pyrite — he was able to make these but not able to commercialize it.
- Jack Rabbit repellent
- Kerosene (petroleum) burner that was effective and ecologically sound — made for his own use
- Lactose successful until the dairy farmers sold their milk

- cows because it wasn't cost effective
- Lime sulfur
- Lip Balm
- Mata Gusanos (worm poison) Creolina
- Muton (rat poison)
- Ointments to fill prescriptions written by Dr Salas and Dr Hatch
- Other fruit flavors — orange, lemon, grape, strawberry, banana, pineapple, etc.
- Packaged leaves and roots from medicinal plants
- Pimple ointment Espinicida
- Pink eye solution for cattle
- Poison wheat for the crows
- Potato chips
- Rauchfleisch for personal use
- Sarnol for sarna (fungicide for mange/itch)
- Shoe polish and cans for it
- Shaving soap
- Sulfa powder in capsules, (Dad encapsulated the powder)
- Vanilla
- Vinegar
- Water softener
- Wax for grafting fruit trees

List of product that Alois unsuccessfully tried to make:

- Puffed wheat
- Polyethylene bottles
- Ceiling tiles out of cement and wood shavings

Appendix 4

The Schill Vanilla Story

Written by Gerhard Schill

Alois Schill came to Mexico from Germany in 1926 with pharmaceutical and chemistry training in order to work with some countrymen who owned the Botica Central in Chihuahua City. Eventually he came to Nuevo Casas Grandes and set up a drugstore, Botica Regional, with a partner. He established the first and only lactose plant in Mexico (to our knowledge). This plant operated until the dairymen sold their cows. He then became the licensed pharmacist for drugstores in the area and made their medicines, among them a salve from a formula of Dr Ernest Leroy Hatch — the well-known Dr Hatch Salve was used to heal cuts and sores.

Alois also ventured to make household and farm products; he furnished embalming fluid to the mortuaries; he made distilled water for the hospitals, the fruit packers and service stations; and he made a variety of other things: bread, potato chips, puffed wheat, detergent, shoe polish, insecticide, lotion 'Crema Liz', flavorings, Bordeaux mixture for fruit trees, etc.

Around 1950 he began studying vanilla making and investigating different formulas, making vanilla in small batches. It became popular with some of the Colonists and was taken to the United States and parts of Mexico. The vanilla business continued to grow.

Gerhard, oldest son of Alois, continued making some of the things his father had made, but over time focused on vanilla. Alois had kept all his formulas in a binder, including the formula for the vanilla. A favorite story is that one time the binder could not be found. Ursula, Alois' wife, knew Gerhard needed the vanilla formula and standing in the kitchen she said aloud, *Ali, if you want us to continue making vanilla, you need to tell us where the binder is*. She then was impressed to go to the hall closet, and pulled out the binder from where Gerhard had hidden it several months earlier in the summer.

Gerhard has continued to make vanilla, even though he feels that someday he will be held responsible for all the addicts. He advises customers to only use a small amount in their recipes and tells them that the vanilla has an obvious expiration date — when the bottle is empty.

Dad and Greg making Vanilla, Gerhard making Vanilla, Vanilla kitchen 2004.

Acknowledgements

I am truly indebted to Mary Ann who allowed me the many hours and days to work on this and her help in sorting pictures and letters. There are many others without whom I would never have completed this. To name a few — Susan Rider, whose book *Journey to Genesee* first planted the seeds for this. My three grown children, Greg, Jennie, and Theresa for their encouragement along the way. Gerhard and Carol Schill for their continued encouragement and supplying material and pictures (even scanned ones), and valuable edits; Gerhard was able to remember some things better than I. To Max Schill, my cousin, who sent me a collection of letters written by my dad to his sister Marie and his father. Max had the foresight to retrieve these from my cousin, Franz, who was getting ready to throw them out when his father, my uncle, passed on. To Max's wife, Anita, for her interest in the Schill relationships and for her help in many ways including bringing relatives together for meetings. To Werner Schill who retrieved schooling information for me and for bringing relatives together for meetings. To my nieces, nephews, and cousins who provided bits and pieces of pictures and notes. To Hermann Baur, my cousin, who provided invaluable information on my mother. To Wolfgang Ertle, my cousin, for his invaluable help in tracking down information. To Ann Schill who provided pictures and information.

   I thank the Mormon Community in Colonia Dublan and Colonia Juarez, who were always kind and helpful to me and afforded me a grade school and high school education and the opportunity to continue my education at BYU in the United States. Without their support, I probably would never have come to the States and made my home here, would probably never have worked for the great companies that hired me. Marathon Oil, Hewlett Packard, and Agilent Technologies gave me the opportunity to work and travel in Germany. This allowed me to improve my German and to travel to my parents' towns and meet our many relatives.

To my mother, for her courage to cross the big ocean to start a new life with my father — not knowing what her future might bring. To my mother and father for their collection of pictures and for getting me started on the right path through their sacrifices, their example and actions. They taught me values, ethics, and an exceptional work ethic.

Andrew Jobling, whose writing class I took, answered many of my writing questions and encouraged me all the way.

To Merryl Scott, my editor, who was a joy to work with and who helped me tremendously. I also want to thank the entire JoJo Publishing team for working with me and making this a pleasant and rewarding experience.

Epilogue

If you have stayed with me this long, you are to be commended and I thank you. This memoir contains what I chose to tell and was done to the best of my knowledge. If I left something important out or if I happened to tell something that was not quite accurate, I ask your forgiveness.

The lives of my parents were merely a small snippet in time. They lived their lives long enough to see all their grandchildren. Now I am a grandparent and am enjoying my three grandchildren. And time continues to tick along. Soon our children will be grandparents and their children will someday be grandparents. Just as my parents are gone, someday I too, will be gone. Such is life, and our next generations will continue into time.

I hope that the effort that I have put into this story of my parents will be passed on to the next generations, and that hopefully they will continue to keep the story going. I sincerely hope that this was worth writing. The last thing I would want to hear when I am gone is for one of my great, great grandchildren to wonder why I bothered. I am very proud of my heritage and my parents, and I hope that pride will continue in the line of their descendants. They made huge sacrifices to give their children opportunities for a better life. They did not have easy lives; but they instilled principles in their children that anyone should be proud of. I only hope that I have instilled those same principles in my children and in all those whose lives I have touched.

www.ingramcontent.com/pod-product-compliance
Lightning Source LLC
Chambersburg PA
CBHW040324300426
44112CB00021B/2871